**United States Holocaust
Memorial Museum**

Phaidon Press Ltd
2 Kensington Square
London W8 5EZ

First published 1995

© 1995 Phaidon Press Limited

ISBN 0 7148 2939 0

A CIP catalogue record for
this book is available from
the British Library.

Printed in Singapore

United States Holocaust Memorial Museum
James Ingo Freed

Adrian Dannatt
ARCHITECTURE IN DETAIL

1

2

3

1, 2 United States Holocaust
Memorial Museum, bridge
through the Tower of Victims.
3 Looking towards the
Education/Conference Center at
concourse level, with its mural of
tiles designed by schoolchildren.
4 View through the bridge
on the third floor, through panes
of glass etched with names of
victims of the Holocaust.

It is not what they built. It is what they knocked down.
It is not the houses. It is the spaces between the houses.
It is not the streets that exist. It is the streets that no longer exist.
James Fenton, A German Requiem

A necessary problem

The opening paragraph of a text such as this has to contain the caveat that it is impossible to write about the Holocaust. It is still necessary to quote Adorno: 'after Auschwitz to write a poem is barbaric'[1] or Steiner's equally obligatory notion that 'in the presence of certain realities art is trivial or impertinent'. [2]

If writing is impossible after the Holocaust, designing buildings about it or writing about such buildings seems all the more problematic. This critique is still in evidence: the film *Schindler's List* was attacked for turning the events into entertainment. Claude Lanzmann, the director of *Shoah*, claimed Steven Spielberg encouraged his audience to cry and that tears in themselves are a pleasure. So austere a reaction is appropriate to the Holocaust, the central problem of the twentieth century and the most important, unanswerable question posed about human nature. But if next to the elegant arguments of Adorno or Lanzmann we stack a mounting pile of cheap revisionist tracts, pamphlets stating the Holocaust never happened, photographs of Nazis in contemporary Germany, desecrated synagogues and Jewish graveyards, a counter argument seems equally appropriate.

What matters is that the truth about the Nazis should never be suppressed or forgotten. To ensure this large numbers of people have to be engaged, moved, informed, even if the means of doing so resembles popular entertainment. The American TV series *Holocaust* was derided as a schlock abomination, but in West Germany it was a revelation, the first time these issues were addressed to and by the majority of people. The screening of *Holocaust* is now considered a significant date in German social history, a moment of transformation in ordinary people's attitudes. The Holocaust cannot be limited to either/or: either factual severity or nothing. It demands both/and: both populist enlightenment and serious scholarship. It is too important to be left just to élitist intellectuals or the mass media; everyone should be a part of it and it should be part of communal memory.

The danger of the Holocaust being forgotten or denied is too real for subtlety. Those who attack *Schindler's List* as pop entertainment miss the point; the Holocaust can survive such pleasures. The opposite of Adorno might even be true, that the event is strong enough to withstand all levels of representation, the more the better. We are now beyond the simple platitude that the Holocaust should not be given physical form or expression. Such icy logic begins to look like 'Good Taste' – a particularly dangerous form of Modernist probity. A building, a poem, song or film, however populist, is surely always better than the elegant silence of superiority when it comes to dealing with the Holocaust and those today who still promote it under disguise of denying it.

4

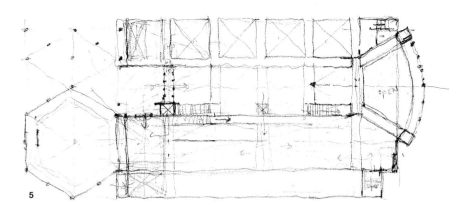

5

6

7

These are not abstract arguments but integral to the design of the United States Holocaust Memorial Museum, and it is from these very issues that the architecture of the museum stems. Conversation with James Freed is not going to be about details of girders but the ideas his building embodies, philosophical problems 'built in' to this project. Freed has managed to engage exactly these issues, to be populist whilst reverent, didactic whilst universal, making them the basis of the design.

The difficulty of writing a book in lieu of a building – a 'souvenir' in the French sense – is more complex when that structure is specifically about the nature of memory – the memory of the attempted destruction of the 'People of the Book', whose religion is based more on a holy text, and its continual interpretation, than on physical buildings.

So it is with trepidation that one presents this text about a building which stands in for a larger, religious text, in itself a kind of building, a temple of words. In Judaism the Torah is the real temple, the text takes the place of the synagogue, not least because a book is transportable, memorizable, unlike a building.

Structure of memory

The Holocaust Memorial Museum was an initiative of President Carter. The Holocaust Memorial Council was set up in 1980 by a unanimous Act of Congress. The Council was mandated to construct 'a permanent living memorial museum to the victims of the Holocaust'; this was to be built on

Federal land transferred to the Council. In 1986 James Ingo Freed was invited to try and amend the scheme of a previous architect, whose plan was thought to be too fascistic. As it had been officially described: 'It was almost brutal. You could not escape identifying it with the architecture favoured by Hitler. It seemed to be more a memorial to the perpetrators of the crime, not the victims.'[3] This suggests an obvious peril of such a project, to manipulate the heroic neo-classicism of the surrounding area of Washington without totalitarian implications. Freed realized the previous plan was unsalvageable and expressed an interest in designing the building. After a number of interviews, he was able to begin his own design and, in 1987, the Federal Fine Art Commission approved Freed's design; in 1988 President Reagan dedicated the cornerstone.

Construction took over four years and the building was inaugurated by President Clinton on the Day of Remembrance, 23 April 1993. Thus on the exterior walls of the Hall of Witness are engraved quotations from these three Presidents, along with the words of Dwight D Eisenhower, Supreme Commander of the Allied Forces, after whom the surrounding plaza is named.

Museums and monuments to the Holocaust are no longer rare; they form a specific genre of architecture and artwork with its own documentation. Indeed, there may even be a certain world-weary resistance to their proliferation – to quote the Israeli poet Yehuda Amichai: 'Pardon me, where can I find the public forgetinal?'[4]

8

9

5 Early plan by James Ingo Freed.
6, 7 Hall of Remembrance: limestone panel on the exterior wall (6); inside the Hall is to be found a calm, empty space where an Eternal Flame burns (7).
8, 9 Permanent exhibition areas by Ralph Applebaum Associates: the ridge beams are original and came from the Auschwitz-Birkenau camp (8); as is the railway car (9, left), a gift to the museum from the Polish government.

10

11

12

Whether we refer to Yad Vashem in Israel or the Beit Hashoah Museum of Tolerance at the Simon Wiesenthal Center in Los Angeles, the question remains the same: how to elucidate without lapsing into entertainment and give form to the act of memory. Although showing artefacts along with text, photographs and documentation, these are essentially buildings conceived to hold a lack, an absence, the missing millions of European Jewry. The paradox of creating a structure to symbolize destruction cannot be resolved simply by presenting ruins or shards – an incongruous Late Romantic gesture. Any such building must show the human capacity for barbarism and vandalism whilst proving, once again, that we are also capable of creativity and construction.

How will these buildings, or their archaeological ruins, be interpreted in three millennia, when the Holocaust may have faded into prehistory? How will their forms explain the Holocaust and suggest the magnitude of the event? Architecture is about time as well as space, temporal as well as spatial duration and transformation. How a building maintains its intention through time, then, is all the more relevant to a museum with the purpose of preventing an event's repetition.

As Frances A Yates proposes in *The Art of Memory*, there is a close connection between architecture and recollection, the use of buildings to prompt memories. Orators of ancient Rome memorized their speeches by identifying them with a building and mentally walking through this space.

In an analogous manner, James Ingo Freed's building could be read, element by element, as a history of the Holocaust; cumulative details forming a grammar of history, an overtly literal structure of memory. But this would reduce the complexity of the building to a single system, a formal reading contrary to its deliberate ambiguity, its confusion of potential metaphors and its overlapping levels of signification.

The design of the Holocaust Memorial Museum is consciously more complex than any so literal a reading. The museum is a montage rather than collage, in which the separate elements are positioned in relation to one another, to afford sequential development, instead of simply a static and isolated juxtaposition for its own sake.

James Ingo Freed

Freed was born in 1930 in Essen, Germany. He and his younger sister moved first to France and later to Switzerland to escape the Nazis, finally settling in Chicago in 1939. Freed studied at the Illinois Institute of Technology under Mies van der Rohe, who remained a lasting influence. Ironically, the Holocaust touches everything, even the aesthetics of a master teacher like Mies, whose position in Nazi Germany led to shades of complicity. Suffice to say that in the complex and anecdotal history of Mies van der Rohe's business relation to the Nazi regime there is sufficient ambiguity to make clear the futility of assigning ideological correlatives to tectonic form.[5]

10–12, 15 James Ingo Freed with I M Pei & Partners, earlier designs: FAA Air Traffic Control Tower, 1972 (10); 88 Pine Street, New York, 1973 (11); Mission Bay, San Francisco, 1982 (12); National Bank of Commerce, Lincoln, Nebraska, 1976 (15).
13, 14 Points of comparison – other memorial and historical museums: the zig-zagged plan of Daniel Libeskind's Berlin Jewish Museum (13) and Yad Vashem museum in Jerusalem (14).

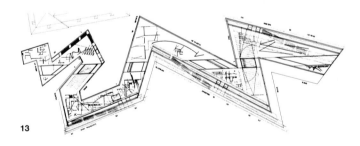
13

14

15

16

17

Freed moved to New York to work with Mies and Philip Johnson on the Seagram Building, although according to legend he fell out with Johnson over its fountains. He arrived at Pei's office in 1956, working briefly as design architect for a project to redevelop the SW Washington Complex, a downtown black ghetto – a very different experience of the capital from his museum. Pei's office was at the height of its success with the legendary developer Zeckendorf, and even the youngest staff were expected to start designing buildings immediately.

At University Plaza, Freed's project begun in 1960, three 30-storey towers are set off sharply against each other with a strong sense of drama against the low-rise surroundings of SoHo.

This student housing still looks elegant today, all the more impressive considering the locality has turned from industrial wasteland to expensive real estate. What was once presumably a brutalist echo of SoHo's factories has gentrified itself along with the area, resulting in an exercise in waffle-like grid geometry. Picasso's bust of Sylvette makes evident the French Late Modernism these towers are in love with, that cool Corb *moderne* now nostalgically revived. This distinctly European quality is to be found again in Freed's museum, while there is also a sensuality in the use of concrete as specific material which could be traced from University Plaza to the carefully deployed, particularly judicious materials of the museum. In the play of natural light on the surface of the towers, an extraordinary visual richness is granted by simple materials, an effect equally evident at the museum.

In 1979 Freed took overall responsibility for another Manhattan scheme, the Jacob K Javits Convention Center on the West Side Highway which suffered a series of near terminal setbacks. Freed's original conception of a transparent, user-friendly amenity never materialized, not least due to continual compromises and alterations. But the Javits, opened in 1986, does have undeniable power, albeit of a bleak and cold nature, not far from the 'polished crystal' of Mies' Friedrichstrasse Office project. It is not hard to imagine that elements of cruelty at play in the Holocaust Memorial Museum were learnt from the totalitarian aspects of Javits; not just its implacable, hostile exterior, but also the necessarily totalitarian task of organizing such large numbers of people.

Any convention centre demands military analogies, a terminology of rallies, speeches, mass psychology. Despite all Freed's attempts to lighten the monumental scale, the Javits is not a place for humanism or the individual, it is a processing machine to move crowds of people in and out, to order. Javits did, however, demonstrate Freed's talent for axial and spatial dynamics, key aspects of the Holocaust Memorial Museum itself. Furthermore, the museum's brilliant organization of the flow of visitors is indebted to the lessons of the Javits Center's fluid circulation. The following description of the Javits Center could almost serve for the museum: '... multiple levels and axes, each separated according to function and threaded through the building in such a way as to emphasize movement through the sequential unfolding of clearly organized layers of space.'[6]

18

19

20

16 James Ingo Freed, I M Pei & Partners, Potomac Tower, Rosslyn, Virginia, 1988.
17 Mies van der Rohe's Friedrichstrasse Office Building project, 1929.
18 James Ingo Freed, design associate, I M Pei & Partners, University Plaza, New York, 1966.
19, 20 James Ingo Freed, I M Pei & Partners, Jacob K Javits Convention Center (19), and Jacob K Javits Convention Center Plaza (20), New York, 1986.

21   22

23

Also the opportunity to design such completely empty space as a convention center, to think on that scale, had its positive effect. The luxurious voids of the Hall of Witness and Hall of Remembrance, their fearless deployment of expensive nothingness, would only seem permissible to someone who had the experience of playing with a total of 1.6 million square feet of space and the world's largest exhibition hall under a single roof, of 410,000 square feet.

In contrast to the anonymity of the Javits Center, the plaza Freed designed there is almost a gesture of atonement, its fountain hinting at the vocabulary of the museum. This park suggests the ludic element missing from the Javits Center, the effect Freed hoped for of 'an elephant dancing on its toes'.

This analogy seems comparable to the work of sculptor Joel Shapiro and his anthropomorphic abstractions which clearly resemble dancing figures much as their austerity denies any such reading. Indeed, Shapiro's ambiguous place between minimalism and figuration shares the museum's aesthetic of both/and rather than either/or. Shapiro's two-part cast bronze sculpture *Loss and Regeneration* activates the entry to the museum on Dwight Eisenhower Plaza, and in which humanity, rather than an elephant, is 'dancing on its toes' – for its life. Freed, widely knowledgeable and supportive of the visual arts, has in all his work found a balance between the necessities of a given form and the expressive potential of its elements. This sculptural and almost literal sense of balance culminates in the Holocaust Memorial Museum.

The site

Washington, DC is a chain of symbols and monuments, producing a very American awe segueing into entertainment. Though all monuments are meant to be symbolic they seem oddly more so in Washington. Like Maya Lin's Vietnam Memorial Wall, that black granite coda, the Holocaust Memorial Museum uses abstract grandeur for its own, bleak story. That the heroic, the 'noble' in scale and material, can be reversed to represent the abject is the source of popularity of both Lin's wall and Freed's museum; and this in itself requires an abstract language based on identifiably classical grammar, principles beloved of early Modernist architects, and from the Parthenon to *pilotis*.

The museum is located just off Washington's central symbolic–historic axis, firmly linking the experience of European Jewry to key events in the foundation of the United States. On a 1.7 acre lot, occupying a total of 258,000 square feet, the museum has to look as if it belongs and yet impose itself as a major new building. It must become assimilated whilst maintaining its own values, be part of society whilst unique and resolutely independent.

The Holocaust Memorial Museum presents a fractured connection to the city line; what at first appears harmonious, an exercise to delight contextualists, begins to display its incongruity. Such tension is produced by exactly an emphasis on congruity, exaggerated conservatism bordering the uncanny.

21–24 James Ingo Freed, recent work at Pei Cobb Freed & Partners: Los Angeles Convention Center, 1993 (21); First Bank Place, Minneapolis, 1992 (22); Federal Triangle, Washington, DC, 1990–5 (projected completion) – a virtually neo-classical style multi-use centre, neighbouring a series of classical buildings (23); San Francisco Main Public Library, 1992–5 (projected completion) (24), which complements San Francisco's Civic Center, an early twentieth-century City Beautiful Movement work.

24

25

The horror of the Holocaust was not of a bizarre, sudden act of violence, but one stemming from everyday life, from ordinary acts of organized, continuous existence, as if part of normality rather than gross aberration. It would have been easy to produce a shocking building, a work which broke with its surroundings, but that would turn the 'banality of evil' into a radical, spectacular act.

Here, at the Holocaust Memorial Museum, Freed has instead taken the repressive tension of the site, the straitlaced formality of the flanking buildings, and further heightened them, to create a sense of unbearable compression, as if the malevolent energy of the museum were held down tightly in place. The repressed is most potent when trying hardest to appear well behaved.

Both limestone and brick
The museum has two older buildings on either side. The essence of the scheme was selecting materials to link clearly the museum to these other buildings. Choosing between brick or limestone Freed used both, the Victorian brick of the Auditors' Building to the north and neo-classical limestone of the Bureau of Engraving and Printing to the south. Hence the museum appears as an extension of these buildings and yet marks a break between them, as the Holocaust is both part of the twentieth century and an unbridgeable dislocation within it. The museum's brick towers continue the forms of the Auditors' Building whilst making clear their own reference to death camps.

Thus an American governmental office is linked by association to the Nazis, as if the processes of administration and control cannot be kept entirely distinct – a building that is simultaneously camp tower and Auditors' office can only be critical.

Between the brick walls of the Holocaust Memorial Museum and the brick walls of the Auditors' Building is a thin alley – a threatening, dangerous passage. Typical of Freed's detailing, the alley is lit by a row of the standard metal lamps used within. This provides a logical method of lighting, yet makes the path more, not less, ominous. It is eerier with the lamps on rather than off. When in use at night the wall looks very European, in the way a fashionable Washington bistro might so wish; brick and lamps together have a distinctly foreign flavour.

But this is the Europe of Céline, of Paul Celan, not Colette. As a more humane counterpoint, trees have been planted along this alley, forming another type of memorial, reminiscent of Joseph Beuys' work, specifically his planting of trees as symbols of resistance and recollection within Kassel.

On the other side, the museum's limestone echoes the formal pomposity of the Bureau of Engraving and Printing, but the Hall of Remembrance's abstract, empty planes instead of columns and windows, suggest an end-game to such a style, a full stop. The hexagonal Hall resembles an exclamation point to the extremely long facade of the neighbouring Bureau building, and it brings not just the Bureau, but the whole tradition of architecture to a close.

26

27

25 The Vietnam Memorial Wall by Maya Lin, with the Washington Monument in the background.
26 Washington's National Mall, view from the Washington Monument looking down towards the United States Capitol.
27 View of the Washington Monument with the Lincoln Memorial to the left.

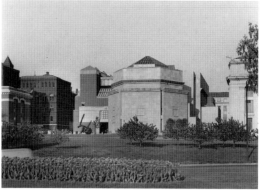

28

29

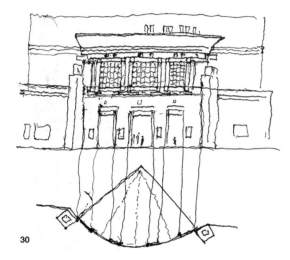

30

The Hall of Remembrance is both of the genre of classicism and yet a refutation of it, a prayer closed in on itself, against the narratives of power and supremacy that neo-classicism implies. Where these stone planes fail to meet, where thin strips of sandblasted glass interrupt, there are recesses at ground level. These are lit from within at night. Stone recesses with the Presidents' words carved upon them,[7] take the place of doors and suggest an enclosed space, something blocked from view or trapped within. There are suggestions in these empty stone planes, as in the brick towers, not only of the camps but also of the ghettos, evoking Venice's Ghetto Nuovo of 1515 with its high walls, outward facing openings bricked shut, and gates which were controlled by Christian guards.

Thus we have brick towers which are obviously symbolic yet of direct continuity with the buildings next to them; we have a limestone facade which continues the appearance of its neighbour whilst bringing it to resolution; and between them we have a set of bridges which are fundamentally metaphoric but in practice join these opposite sides.

As a basic plan the museum resembles a catamaran, one wing in brick, the other in limestone, held together by steel bridges. Between them lies the moral marrow of the structure, the Hall of Witness. Nazi revisionists claim that there were no gas chambers at Auschwitz-Birkenau, that the chimneys, crematoria and blocks with no windows were an industrial complex. Freed has taken this lie and reversed it. He has created a civic monument with many of the tectonic elements of the camps for no practical purpose, only

remembrance. Revisionists insist that these places were only factories, that the buildings could be explained. Freed has made a factory that cannot be explained, a factory producing nothing but history.

Two entrances

The Holocaust Memorial Museum is located between 14th and 15th Street and has an entrance on both sides. It is on 14th that coach parties, schoolchildren and the majority of visitors enter, and it has a grand portico, a 'prow' of Indiana limestone. Yet the real entrance is on the other side, facing the park and quiet vista of 15th Street. At least this is the 'real' entrance for myself and those who might find the other too bombastic or unnecessarily proclamative for its purpose. Likewise the visitor impressed by 14th Street, who thinks a large, declamatory entrance necessary for a major museum, might find the 15th Street doors far too modest and ordinary.

From compromise Freed has made a virtue, giving us not one building and programme, but several overlapping, mutually inclusive buildings and readings. Freed provides two entrances we can all appreciate, depending on our history and sensibility, one no more privileged than the other.

When President Clinton opened the building he used the forecourt of 15th Street. There would not have been room on 14th Street, the portico reaches right out to the kerb and it would not have seemed appropriate. Such large, symbolic architecture demands a President be centre-stage, between the two giant pillars with their out-of-scale lamps at the top. This would have

28, 31 United States Holocaust Memorial Museum, 14th Street elevation.
29, 32 United States Holocaust Memorial Museum, 15th Street elevation.
30 Sketch of the 14th Street elevation by James Ingo Freed.
33 The alley between the museum and the neighbouring Auditors' Building, lit by lamps also used within the museum itself.

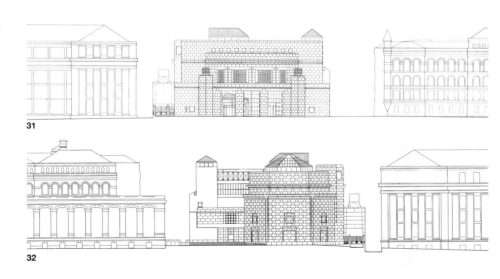

31

32

33

34

35

36

suggested, especially from a photographic angle, dictatorial control, rallies, the full pomp of state power. Neo-classical symmetry only needs a single figure of power, isolated equidistantly, to become dangerous. By contrast, it is immediately democratized by crowds of people; in the presence of hundreds of milling tourists, it dissolves in use amongst a flow of individuals. Where the President made his speech there was no sense of his being framed, centered by the museum behind him; the 15th Street approach is deliberately anti-symmetrical and inherently democratic. With its shy, almost concealed doors, its stepped, jagged levels and the skewed planes of the Hall of Remembrance the entrance is disorientating not triumphant.

Freed has imbued Eisenhower Plaza with an unease comparable to Venturi, Scott Brown and Associates' stairway at London's National Gallery extension, altered because of its sensation of an almost certain tumble. This psychological effect is emphasized by Shapiro's sculpture: a sprawling, tripping figure, which could be the visitor, fooled by the descending levels. The second part is all the more remarkable: a house balanced on its roof, blown over by a cataclysm, whose metal interior rings suitably hollow, positioned right by the pavement, close to the road; a banal shape, a Monopoly dwelling, overturned as if natural order had been reversed. This is Freed's theme, one of transforming ordinary structures into something disquieting, making the quotidian sinister not by subversion but by over-identification.

From 15th Street one is immediately confronted by Shapiro's up-ended house, a counterpoint to the Hall of Remembrance behind it. Then one mounts the broad incline of steps ('steppes' might be appropriate) to Shapiro's other figure, a symbol of fallen humanity. This approach is slow – three brick levels ensure that – and one does not draw any closer to a centralized portal. One must change direction and shift to the right. There, hidden in the shadow of the Hall's hexagon, are two rotating doors. In fact, both entrances are equally modest: 14th Street proclaims itself a glorious atrium but dwindles to rotating doors within a guard house.

The portico on 14th Street is a fake, just a curved facade, a screen with a gap open to the sky behind it. We move from the declamatory to the ordinary, from light to shade, preparing for the journey. We wait in a shallow courtyard to gain entry to another courtyard, then another – a triple reorientation. This complexity continues throughout, inspiring awe in us with the size of the project yet at the same time apologizing for doing so. Entering via 14th street we expect a straightforward, classical interior plan, instead of which we come to a semi-circle lined with flags, a curved space that moves us on into the Hall of Witness. We keep expecting to be stopped, asked for a ticket, proof of entering the museum proper. On entering nobody would notice the discreet side corridor, the only means of entrance to the fifth floor, reserved for visitors by appointment.

By use of design, the sweep of the curved entry, one is immediately led onwards, past this passage, maintaining the privacy of that floor without being élitist or exclusionary. Neither entry, discreet or populist, 15th or 14th Street, prepares the visitor for the psycho-geographic maze within.

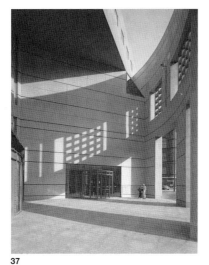

37

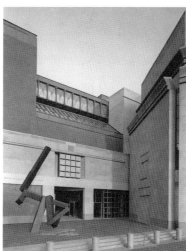

38

34 Sketch of 15th Street elevation by James Ingo Freed.
35 15th Street entrance showing Joel Shapiro's two-part cast bronze sculpture, *Loss and Regeneration*.
36 View of bridge and roofs with the Washington Monument beyond.
37, 38 The two entrances: 14th Street's curved entrance portico (37) and the 15th Street entrance (38) with its broad, stepped incline.

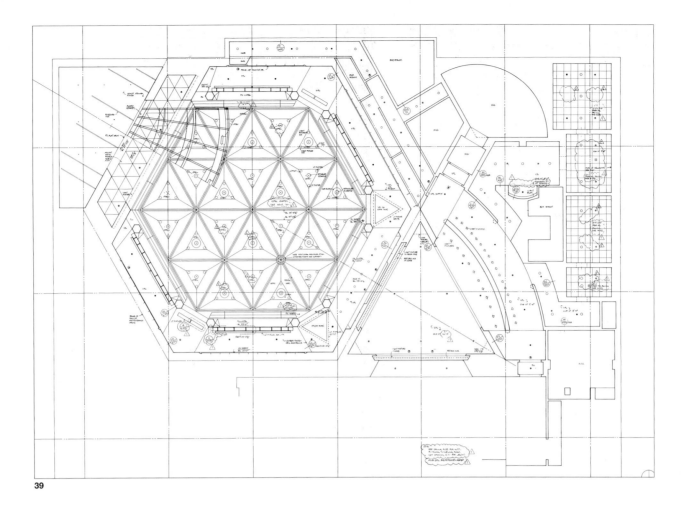

39

40

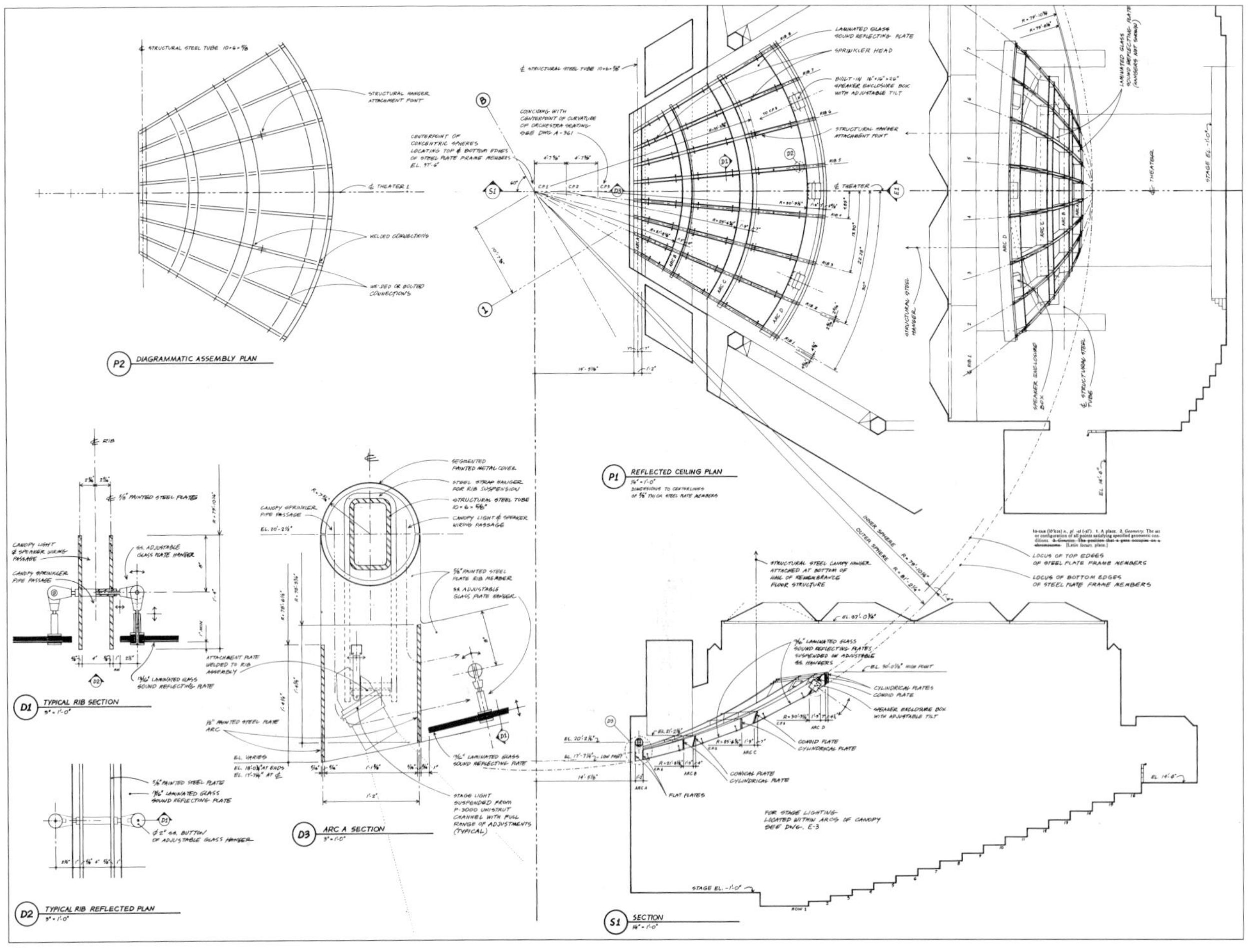

39, 40 United States Holocaust Memorial Museum drawings: reflected ceiling plan (39) and acoustic canopy details (40) of the Meyerhoff Theater, accessed at concourse level.

41   **42**

Public memorial and private museum

If from without the building is both brick and limestone, industrial and neo-classical, this division continues within, a mixture of public memorial space and the separate programme of the permanent exhibition. Thus the two Halls and connecting galleries, staircases and walkways are in the public domain, whilst the exhibition keeps to itself. That Freed's building is both memorial and museum is made clear by its division, with the actual museum so self-contained that it is possible to walk around the rest of the building without realizing it is there.

The permanent display occupies three floors. It could be read as the building's generator or motor, an engine room, integral to the operation of a building, but not necessarily the first thing one sees; just a functional box taking up the south wing, though exhibitions also carry through some sections of the north wing. The permanent exhibition occupies 40,000 square feet and has a potential total five hours of reading material and five hours of audiovisual material. But the building also contains two theatres, a library, archive, conference centre and administrative offices.

When I first visited the building I felt I had access to all areas. I was describing a circle, I could loop the building whilst never getting to the museum itself. This means the building becomes a communal space, an open-air park, which keeps the whole alive. Thus one can spend a day within the 'memorial' precincts without touring the 'museum' rooms at all. Yet the two are interdependent; the darkness and claustrophobia of the exhibition

and its contents transform the experience of the building, making it brighter by relief, blacker by association. The visitor, however, cannot go round the permanent exhibition without retracing a path through the space. If at first the associations of the Hall of Witness are not evident, they become so traversing the bridges across it, going from one side of the exhibition to the other.

Visitors are threaded, from one to another, across the Hall of Witness; the paths of so many pedestrians, as if in time-delay photography, knitting a web of experience to hang above it. The spatial complexity and ambiguity of the normally highly systematic museum-going process stems from Freed's personal freedom with this project. The museum changed Freed's attitude towards architecture. This was one building he could take chances with, aware that architects don't like taking chances, and when they do, they often take silly ones. Certain of Freed's attitudes became more predominant, moving away from fixed architectural 'solutions', trying rather to work his way into the theme of a building before deciding where the necessary, if more banal, elements would go. Freed wanted idiosyncrasy, a more irrational, non-Bauhaus method. He even went through the drawings of the architects on the design team removing anything that might have been considered a neat resolution, to keep difficulties intact, the space problematized.

Every visitor to the museum, whatever his itinerary, is going to traverse his own path, crossing previous lines of locomotion. If this can suggest a rat trapped in an experiment, unable to locate an escape, it also ensures

43

44   **45**

41, 42 Below the exhibition spaces and Halls: The Helena Rubinstein Auditorium (41) and The Joseph and Rebecca Meyerhoff Theater (42), both at concourse level.
43 Sketch of the 15th Street elevation by James Ingo Freed.
44, 45 Above the exhibition spaces: library areas, fifth floor.

46

47

that one experiences the entire spatial variety, the fullness of the building, whether one wants to or not. In a quest to locate the core of the building, the visitor is obliged to reconsider the notion of any singular centre, wandering through a variety of other spaces, spaces which may convey information about the Holocaust without words or photographs.

Hall of Witness

From either entrance one passes through an antechamber, a room for security, baggage and then on into ... what? Into a large, hollow interior which resembles another hall of arrival. It is not clear whether one is already in the building or still trying to enter it. One has come in only to go outside again. Indeed, there is an almost acoustical transformation entering the Hall, an atonal dissonance followed by temporary reassurance of a statement of the main theme. The Hall of Witness is just a gap between two halves of the building, but at the same time it is the break, the caesura the Holocaust requires, the absence it poses. Thus the Hall is both a non-place and the central space, a psychologically empty correlative to the physically empty Hall of Remembrance.

This witness Hall is disturbing and fractured, with elements sloping one way or another, in contradictory directions, forming a pattern of interrupted logic. Freed's design is cruel in its own subtle way, an architectonic version of Nietzsche's belief that: 'Our highest cultural products are expressions of sublimated cruelty.'

From 14th Street one passes through yet one more portal, a single I-beam suspended across two metal poles. This threshold implies one has finally arrived, a grid of angles suggestive of an orientation point, yet the Hall gives no indication of where to proceed. The lack of orientation suggests Freed's experience in the Mapping Service, getting maps up to date, reworking lines. The Hall of Witness is like a map of the Holocaust where all coordinates have been displaced or half-erased, a cartography more threatening than reassuring.

On the east wall are empty panels of white marble slightly grained with pink veins, in direct contrast to the black granite squares of the other end of the Hall. The white is evocative of a certain purity, or the snows of the 1944 death marches. Like Ellsworth Kelly's monochrome panels in the room above it, this wall seems too unsoiled for such an environment; it is as if all 'whiteness' has been gathered at one end of the building.

There are two rows of glass block lit along the floor, a path which ends between two stairways. Like being given a route to discover, it leads to more choice, another directional dilemma. Neither stairway leads to the display if that is what one is, by now, looking for; the one that rises leads to the Hall of Remembrance, the one that descends takes the visitor to the concourse level's lecture theatre, cinema, temporary gallery and classrooms. This glass trajectory crosses next to a public information counter, the only shelter in the empty plain, where people cluster less for advice than for protection from the dizzying agoraphobia of so much open space. The very idea of advice or assistance seems futile in such an environment.

46 Sketch of the towers by James Ingo Freed.
47–49 Views of the Hall of Witness: looking down from the Hall to concourse level (48), and up to the second floor (49). Note the metal lamps also used in the alley outside (47).
The skylight admits sheets of light that vary with the time of day, and that are fragmented by the steel structure through which light passes.

48

49

50

51

This lit flight-path serves less as elucidation than as one more element of confusion, a fissure in the cedar rose granite paving, a gap that could widen instantly. Whilst it neatly divides the building along another diagonal, cutting off housekeeping to one side, the glass line also points to the Washington Monument outside, and a continuity and break with the idealism it represents. The angle perhaps also suggests Oskar Hansen's 1959 proposed monument at Birkenau, a special path of granite to slash diagonally across the grid of the camp.[8]

But most of all this illuminated track suggests the fractures of history, a transparent scar defacing the smooth museum surface, as if, to quote architect Lebbeus Woods: 'Acceptance of the scar is an acceptance of existence.'[9] This scar was originally to have been joined by another one, a crack running down the granite west wall, by the stairs. This split would have made clear – possibly too clear – a sense of the building as a flawed, fractured project, something that should never have been completed and was so by default or obligation.[10] This break would have paid homage to Nikolai Kolli's proposed 1918 Soviet public sculpture, *The Red Wedge*, a pedestal with a crack running through it, although, conversely, it might also have bordered on the facile iconography of James Wines' SITE.

The twin fissures of floor and wall would have made the Hall of Witness an earthquake zone, as in Jean-François Lyotard's description of the Holocaust: 'an earthquake so powerful as to destroy all the instruments of measurement'.[11] In fact a crack down the length of the wall proved not only aesthetically but technically *de trop*. Freed asked sculptor Richard Serra to help create this split, but the material proved intractable. What the polished, premium black granite wall does do is reflect people within the Hall, creating a dark mirror of phantom figures. Serra, however, contributed the boldest art work, as inseparable from the architecture as Shapiro's tumbling overture. He inserted a massive slab of Cor-ten steel into the stairway that leads down from the Hall to concourse level, splitting the steps.

Around this metal wall the visitor is faced with another decision, to go one way or the other, to avoid its headlong violence. The wall is openly cold and cruel, an elemental force that cannot be negotiated with or appeased. Though entirely abstract, people have noted technical numbers at the top and assumed they refer to camp tattoos. It is the nature of Freed's project (but not Serra's) to let such a reading stand, and encourage a plurality of interpretations in place of dogma. Serra's *Gravity* suggests one strategy Freed avoided – that of the Jungian solution of archaic form. Simple shapes carry great weight, and Serra's intervention aspires to the solemnity of the black cube of Mecca. It certainly fulfils Serra's intention: 'In confronting the site I wish to create a field force so that the space is discerned physically rather than optically.'

The artists selected by independent jury for the Holocaust Council – Shapiro, Serra, Sol LeWitt, and Ellsworth Kelly – are all classic Modernists. Like Freed their aim is to generate reflection, emotional rather than intellectual, from a reduced vocabulary of austerity. They do not use

52

53

50, 51 Looking across the Hall of Witness stairs that lead up to the second floor and down to concourse level.
52, 53 Looking lengthwise down the main/first floor with the Hall of Witness to the side.

16

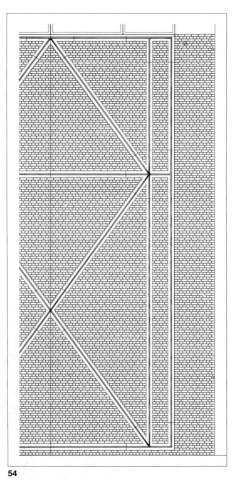

54

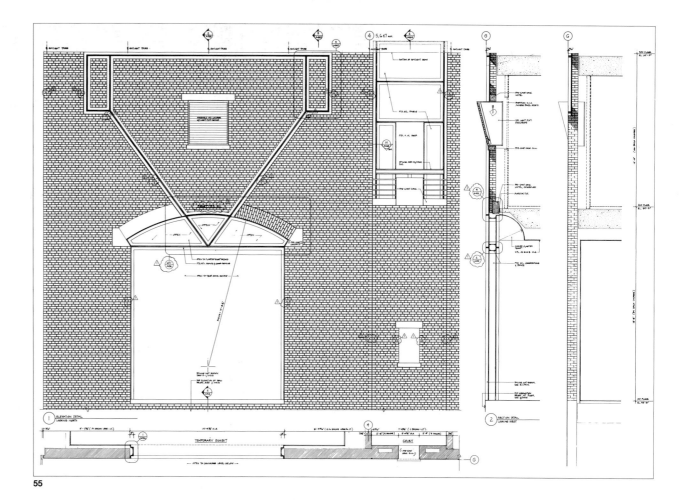

55

54–56 Masonry wall details: typical tower facing Hall of Witness (54); interior brick of Hall of Witness – elevation detail looking north and section details looking west (55); metal cross bracing details (56).

57–59 Art works within the museum: Ellsworth Kelly's *Memorial* (57) and Sol LeWitt's *Consequence* (58) installations at fourth/third and second floor lounges; and Richard Serra's sculpture, *Gravity* (59) by the concourse level stairs.

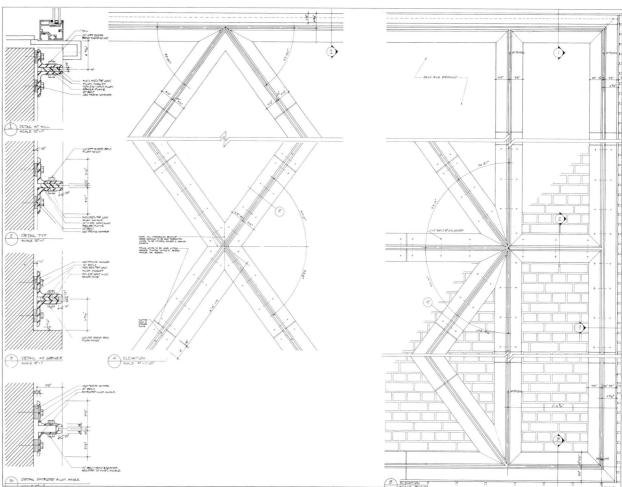

56

57

58

narrative, though Shapiro's introduction of figurative associations into minimalism is close to Freed's own aesthetic. As artists they do not need to provide literal associations – that is their hermetic blessing and curse. Freed's work, however, obliges him to make the building speak, rather than to remain majestically silent. In the Hall of Witness Freed works hardest to balance the abstract, tectonic and narrative. His aim is to remain metaphoric, not symbolic. The building is not symbolic, it is suggestive, and the range of suggestions is wide.

The museum may appear as a decorous container to some and to others as a cruel processing machine, a bland civic monument and simultaneous horror show. Such effects are produced by attention not just to general form but to the smallest details and associations, the most subtle, intimate elements. To misquote his old teacher: here the devil, not God, looms in the details. The details Freed uses go back to something before. Here is a concentration, through Mies, of rigorous tectonics as a devising force, as a means of building. There is an attention to detail, a precise methodology of construction that makes the place memorable. Building becomes architecture by the conscious understanding of putting things together – details, oven doors, ornamental steel, and in particular the use of industrial lamps and moulded brick.

The type of brick took a year to select; these bricks have bumps, pick up light aggressively and are essential to the atmosphere of the building. In his Madison Avenue office Freed displays a single brick from a concentration camp, atop an upright I-beam. The bricks at the museum perform inside and outside with an ambiguous texture that shimmers and disappears. The walls have power, maybe because such brick is rarely used for interiors. They disintegrate in light to magnificent forms destroyed, dissolved by the jagged shards of day. This is particularly evident when they turn beautiful with sunset and begin to glow. Freed's use of brick is logical yet poetic; his own first experience of architecture was the simple pleasure of brick, having been given a little bag of them as a student exercise in his first year at IIT. Mies' over-quoted dictum should not go unquoted in this context either: 'Architecture begins when two bricks are carefully put together'.

The story-telling parts of this Hall are important, yet it is equally vital that everything works, that the brick walls are self-supporting, unlike Renzo Piano's Ircam building in Paris, where bricks are merely elements in a decorative facade held in metal frames. The red brick is warm, tactile yet eventually disturbing. The brick walls of camp ovens are present in ghost form, haunting us by association. This brick is essentially of continental European domestic culture, and is human rather than monumental in scale, but it is also sinister. Freed uses brick like Per Kirkeby's sculpture or Rafael Moneo's National Museum of Roman Art at Mérida, as the fabric of time; but this is a history that can turn sour, that suggests small-town bigotry as well as enlightenment.

This, moreover, is emphasized by the lamps, which in spacing and design imply the camps. Freed understands the potential effect of just a metal lamp

59

60

61

62

60 View from concourse level to bridges at the Hall of Witness.
61 Black granite wall at concourse and first floor level.
62 View down north wall of the Hall of Witness leading into the exhibition spaces.
63 Sketch by James Ingo Freed.

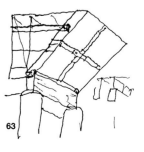

63

64

65

on a brick wall, and that the dark poetry of Magritte can be translated into an architecture of recollection and suggestion. Likewise, high on the walls there are batteries of lights pointing down behind slanted slats which deliberately recall camp lamps, especially as the space is full of daylight and hardly needs such illumination. These slats ajar imply a process of surveillance, eyes upon us, the fake ventilation systems built in the death houses, even the cattle trucks. [12]

Equally decorative and ominous are metal elements embedded in the brick walls, V-shapes, a repeated triangle motif, a section of the Star of David. Variations on this triangle are a discreet, continual presence, making sense as straightforward design, only suggesting a metaphoric content on contemplation. All details add to this unease.

The use of brick bound with metal, the addition of heavy steel to raw wall, is elegant but also recalls the binding of camp ovens, held in place against heat's expansion. The ovens were so overused that they often exploded from the pressure of gasses within. In these metal straps there is a wealth of metaphoric play: of the constraints of history, the enslavement of a people, the compression of physical torture, perhaps even the straps of Tefillin. Equally these horizontal straps of metal could be reminiscent of the *tallit*, the Jewish prayer shawl with its black bands of mourning. These associations never force themselves but linger instead like a suggestive stain. Steel elements used throughout are equally threatening: gates, rails, bars that herd us up and down. The use of steel bars as handrails might even bring up an

association of railway tracks – a not dissimilar form in short sections.

Resting a hand on the metal beam it comes to feel like part of an old European train station; it could even pass as a converted nineteenth-century industrial building. In this way it is close to Aulenti's Musée d'Orsay, a structure of two bridge-linked wings. Similarly, the Washington station where President Garfield was assassinated is now the National Gallery of Art. But the Holocaust Memorial Museum is not a historical building, rather a contemporary structure dealing with history. Trains and stations are central to the Holocaust and there are risks in any such association. [13] It might even be possible to see the overall plan as a gigantic, abstracted detail of a railway track, the bridges as sleepers, the two parallel wings as rails. It may be like a railway station because here people come and go, choose their destination, but it is the opposite in one respect: stations are about symmetry and logic; the Hall of Witness is the reverse. Freed's central reference when designing the Hall of Witness was the brick, end wall at Auschwitz against which people were shot – a simple, empty rectangle.

From within it seems that the Hall is at an angle, apparently anti-symmetrical. Due to the large staircase descending from the west, the base of which spreads out from the top, the entire perspective is altered, and the staircase seems to narrow or expand. Combined with the skylight the stairway creates distortion, a mixed reception. The dominant skylight of exposed structural steel is twisted and buckled; wrenched and turned it is like the Hall, neither inside nor outside.

64, 66 Door and V-shaped motif at Hall of Witness.
65 Skylight detail with view of bridge above.
67 Sketch by James Ingo Freed showing crack originally intended for west wall of Hall of Witness.

66

67

68

69

The Hall of Witness is really an open-air assembly, exterior masquerading as interior. If one lifted up the skylight one would be standing in an empty courtyard, a ghetto alleyway. In Yehuda Amichai's words: 'Like the inner wall of a house / that after wars and destruction becomes / an outer one –'.[14]

The permanent display

There are doors on both sides of the Hall of Witness. To the north, at the base of the towers, is an exhibition for children, 'Daniel's Story'; one entrance, one exit, separated in the middle by a locked door and gate. To reach these doors one must cross short metal bridges with gates, over an interior moat between wall and floor.

On the south side there is the 15th Street exit, a cloakroom, a bookshop, a room containing a roll-call of sponsors, and stairs down to the concourse level. The entrance to the permanent display is also here, with a line of people waiting for elevators. Once fed into the exhibition system, starting from the fourth floor and working down, the process is inexorable, although there are escape routes for those who find it unbearable. The elevators are standard hydraulic models yet generate claustrophobia, with stark lighting, raw metal, low ceilings and a video monitor that plays a short clip of liberators arriving at the camp. A voice intones: 'We don't know what it is; some sort of prison' – almost a description of the museum. The clip stops just as the doors open. The large grey service elevators are even more ominous, their huge doors closing with a groan of finality.

These are not meant to be cattle cars, but people are capable of deducing symbolic intent from the most meagre clues as if this narrative association were a human need withheld by pure abstraction. There is the danger, then, that the building becomes a game of reference spotting, like 'finding' body parts in an abstract painting, with schoolchildren encouraged to 'spot' towers, railway sleepers and oven bricks.[15] The display of exhibits in itself, designed by Ralph Applebaum Associates, is chronological and didactic rather than poetic – the opposite of the building. The process of viewing becomes a re-enactment of the events. Due to a narrow approach the visitor waits, squeezed in line to go through a cattle truck, and the audience flow slows and congeals when it comes to the central, operative moment: the gas chambers. Here the story comes to its impenetrable conclusion; the relief is palpable when one can go on to the next section, and the inevitable exit. It is difficult to speed through the years, or to avoid pressure points where the crowds are forced to gather, pushed through an actual Birkenau 'Pferde-stallbaracken' (horse-stable-barrack), that canonical representation of German camps.[16]

The containment of the bulk of the display to one side, a lightless box, frees the rest of the building and works perfectly with the dynamics of the exhibition. The visitor needs nothing other than a dark, labyrinthine cube; this taut, sprung maze is an ideal analogy to the sequence of events one is forced to watch in strict chronology. After just one floor one hungers for light and space. This need is granted, suddenly and amply.

70

71

68, 69 The exposed structural steel of the skylight.
70 View down the Hall of Witness with bridges leading to temporary exhibition spaces at left.
71 Elevators at Hall of Witness taking the visitor up into the exhibition.

72

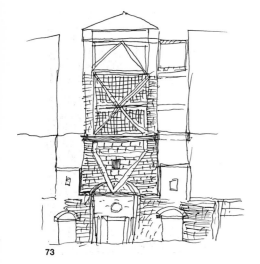

73

Bridges

Freed develops practical solutions which are simultaneously metaphoric resolutions. The use of steel-framed glass bridges to move from one wing to the other is exemplary: they are needed both technically and emotionally, to cross to the other side of the exhibition and to move out from the display. On a corkscrew pattern, the museum works down from fourth, into third, to second floor, using both wings. Moving from one side to the other is achieved via these bridges, the first on the fourth floor engraved with names of destroyed places; the next, on the third floor, of destroyed people. These bridges provide essential light and freedom after the dark alleys of the displays, and one escapes from the enclosure of the camps into sudden sky, a brief passage of freedom.

Their transparency suggests the rationalism of the Enlightenment; with the mildest echo of the Bridge of Sighs they provide a double sigh: relief from the pressures of history as well as sadness at the tale that continues before and after. If these bridges belong to camp observation systems they also suggest ghetto walkways, Nazis isolating people from the 'virus' of Judaism. It is only from the bridges that the full crookedness of the skylight can be understood. What seems a straightforward cube when within it, now reveals itself as twisted, tormented space of alogic. The glass roof buckles and contracts; the plan seems to have come adrift, it is hard to reconcile the two spaces from within and without. It reveals itself as a distorted, ruptured structure, just as the neo-classical foundations of Fascist society seen from the overview of history appear as barbarism, insanity, chaos.

The names of lost towns and people prevent the glass bridges from becoming transcendental, redeeming passageways; they do not allow these otherwise beautiful structures to serve as cathartic escape. The etched names are like the base of Daniel Libeskind's model for the Jewish Museum in Berlin in three dimensions: a layer of text, a sheet of words in memory of lost worlds. Seen with a light spray of Washington drizzle the poetry of these old European syllables becomes bathetic, with the glass roofs beyond evoking an echo to the folkloric refrain. The descent from floor to floor acts as a version of Dante's rings of *Inferno*; his warning 'Lasciate ogni Speranza' (Abandon All Hope) seems a direct predecessor to the notorious gate engraved 'Arbeit Macht Frei'. This concentric descent is also a practical scheme for dividing the museum.

The fourth floor is 'The Nazi Assault 1933–39'. From there one crosses the bridge to walk through the north wing, and the last, Tower of Victims, with its high walls of photographs of the occupants of a *shtetl*, past whom one crosses by bridge. This tower descends to the next floor, visible at the sides. These rooms on the north side, on the fourth and third floors, let in daylight from narrow slots, the only natural lighting allowed in the display.

One then goes down a stairway and through Ellsworth Kelly's *Memorial* of white monochrome shapes, a decompression chamber equivalent in geometric effect to the Hall of Remembrance at the other end of the building. From here one can see down the Hall of Witness from the east, feel for oneself the white marble of the end wall. Having now reached the third floor,

72, 74, 75 Views of bridges. The visitor views the Hall of Witness from above, the names on the glass a constant reminder of lost places and people (72, 75). The bridge with glass walls and floor (74) spans over the Hall of Witness to connect the two sides of the fifth floor library/archives.
73 Tower and bridge sketch by James Ingo Freed.

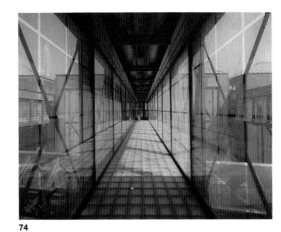

74

75

76　　　　　　　**77**

78

one re-enters darkness for the 'Final Solution 1940–45'. This section ends all the way back at the west at a second bridge, directly underneath the first. Through a sandblasted glass block one sees feet overhead, where one's own feet had been an hour previously. The very act of walking across glass seems foolhardy, like stepping into a void. These two bridges look one way onto the skylight, the other side is a grey wall. As the brick is beautiful by sunset, so the etched names are cast on the pale corridor, forming a pattern of not quite readable letters, a shadow braille of ghost nomenclature. One realizes how exposed one was below and wonders about the bridges above, where they go, who is using them. There is a constant sense of being seen, of the literal overview of observation posts and the overview of history. In Aldo Rossi's phrase: 'Every tower is made for observing, but even more for being observed.'[17]

The other side of the third floor contains Applebaum's exhibition design: a terrible pile of old shoes from the camps, which give off a distinct, unholy odour of death; rows of photographs; tattoos on arms; piles of hair. This section is precise and elegant, influenced by the display of conceptual art and Christian Boltanski's work in particular. Passing through the base of the Tower of Victims, one goes down again. Here stairs become metal, loose and clanky; it is hard to descend without making a loud noise, a deadly rattle. This sound rings hollow like Shapiro's house on the Plaza.

In both Freed's building and Applebaum's exhibition design, there are continually changing materials underfoot, from wood to carpet, carpet to brick, granite to 'Death March' metal – a variety of unsettling textures. The rattle of steel stairs, the hum of lifts, the smell of old shoes: the museum as a whole is as much an auditory, olfactory experience as a visual one. Passing by Sol LeWitt's wall drawing one unfortunately does just that; it seems cramped, unrelated to the story, despite LeWitt's connections to the building: his direct family were Russian Jews; he worked as graphic designer at I M Pei's office from 1955–56.

Descending to the second floor of the exhibition one walks into the gloom of the 'Last Chapter'. From here the exit is not another bridge, but down a ramp next to a wall built from Jerusalem stone, and out directly opposite the Hall of Remembrance which one walks into, is even pulled into, wiping away embarrassed tears. From the Hall of Remembrance a gallery can be crossed to stairs that lead down to the Hall of Witness. A grid of four by four squares, divided by glass, makes a granite window, a mute heraldic shield onto Eisenhower Plaza. Past the stairs, the other wing of the second floor is occupied by the Wexner Learning Center and desks with interactive computers.

The two parallel sections linked by bridges imply a variety of bifurcated themes, past and future, Europe and America. It seems significant that exhibits can only be reached by technology, through lifts, and only exited by foot, walking your way round and out of the narrative. Likewise German technology led to the Holocaust, where engineering was divorced from its Enlightenment origins, which could only be escaped by those who walked across Europe – the most ancient, basic tactic of salvation.

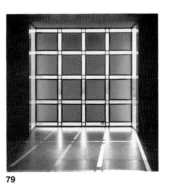

79　　　　　　　**80**

76 Looking towards a bridge and down to the skylight below.
77 Hall of Witness seen from the second floor.
78 Glass block bridge floor.
79, 80 A four by four square granite window gives onto Eisenhower Plaza, here seen from inside and out.

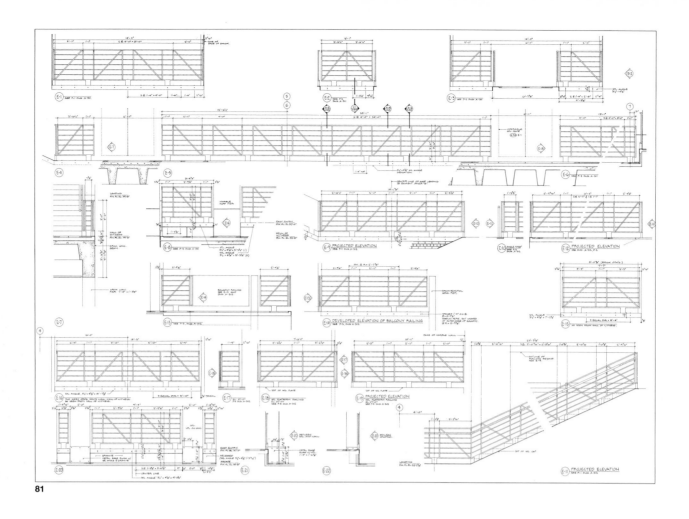

81

22

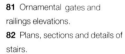

81 Ornamental gates and railings elevations.
82 Plans, sections and details of stairs.

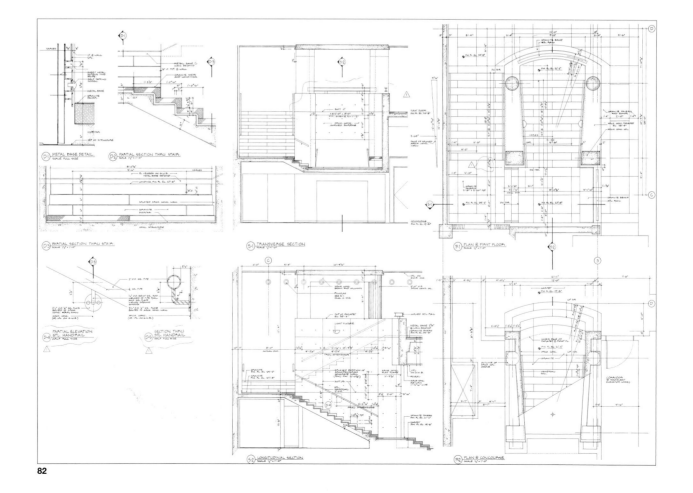

82

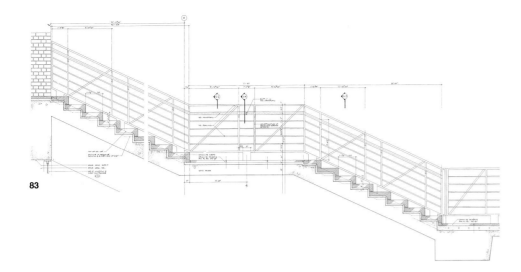

83

Fifth floor

If the towers and pitched metal roofs refer to the Auditors' Building they also pick up geometrical elements from the Washington Monument. This is particularly clear from the fifth floor's archives, library and conference room. Here, with two sides of the Washington Monument visible, the connection between the interior shape of the roofs and the sharpened point of the monument becomes overt. And if the roofs are the apex of the towers, their closest resemblance to the camps, it is suitable that they are reserved for the study of Jewish history. The top floor is reserved for scholars, survivors, and those with academic or personal connections. One tower contains the computerized system linking Holocaust survivors.

Thus the strongest architectural resemblance to the camps is where remembrance takes most potent form. In fact the shape of these roofs is as pleasing from within as it is threatening from without. Inside, there are quiet, elegant offices and libraries, with narrow windows that keep sunlight from the book stacks, the opposite of the claustrophobic rooms underneath. Shapiro's metal house below also echoes these roofs; these are archetypal forms, the basic home a child might draw, here given significant scale and resonance. On the fifth floor are the three central bridges one can see from below. Here the same grey painted steel is used, there is no clear glass: it is stippled with small squares rather than names.

The only disappointment is that the final bridge on the west side could not have been left as purely symbolic: impossible to enter, sealed off as empty space. This would have been quite feasible – three bridges are more than sufficient for the circulation required. The end bridge on the opposite, east side, above the 14th Street entrance, is itself far from being a walkway, and is lined with administrative offices which form a row of separate rooms.

Concourse level

At concourse level the spaces are all the more surprising in their inter-connections, their complex way of moving, flowing. The approach to the temporary exhibition space is particularly threatening. There is a big metal gate, held open, at once both cattle door and jail trapping. The floor switches from grey carpet to red brick; indeed all surfaces are brick, and there is a row of low lamps along the far wall. This route runs from Serra's *Gravity* to a narrow gap, where one looks up to see the metal platform at the east entrance and the beginning of the skylight beams, a hidden beginning for the whole museum.

Freed's combination of suggestive detail and practicality is once more made evident. Here is the lit fissure that runs across the Hall of Witness. Now, however, it is a long strip of fluorescent lighting to illuminate the basement. The lighting works as metaphor above, shining through glass brick, and illumination below. The gap between the Hall of Witness floor and its wall, which one has to cross by small metal bridges, is a distancing device above; below it affords a view and light. Here there are three classrooms and between them large grey metal doors which make overt links to camp ovens.

Freed is not afraid to diminish perfection in the cause of humanity. A whole

84

85

86

83 Section of Hall of Witness stair.
84 Gate at the top of monumental stair.
85 Fifth floor bridges with the Washington Monument beyond.
86 Tower interior, fifth floor study area.

88

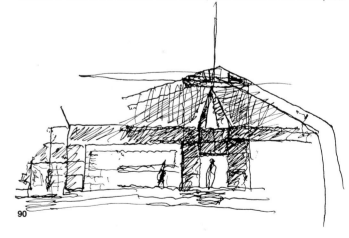

87

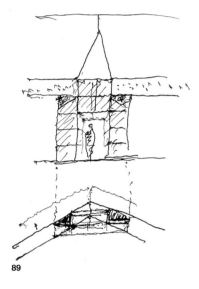

89

wall of the diagonal corridor is taken up with painted, glazed tiles made by schoolchildren. At the 15th Street entrance is a small window. One of the tiles is placed up on the wall, at window level, to suggest what takes place down below: a clear break with the otherwise anonymous elegance of the approach.

Hall of Remembrance

The museum, the Holocaust, the memorial, all end with the Hall of Remembrance. The bible relates how Pompey in Jerusalem barged into the temple, demanding to be shown the Holy of Holies. He was surprised to find himself in an empty room. The presence of the name of God in the Holy of Holies generated a divine radiation, the *Shekhinah*, which destroyed any unauthorized person. This is the Hall of Remembrance.

Here Freed has achieved that rare thing, a genuinely contemporary religious space, without denomination or artefacts. The tranquillity of this space, its organization, is achieved by the walls that hover on each of six sides, forming a counterpoint to Ellsworth Kelly's canvases. They are walls as freestanding plaques. The joins between the walls are replaced by thin windows of sandblasted glass, forming gaps in each corner. There is the straightforward symbolism of the Star of David and six million dead, yet the Hall of Remembrance also operates within the civic fabric of Washington. It is part of the typology of neo-classical monuments, whilst acting as a place of reverence. Freed has created a space that is solemn and religious; yet unlike the Holy of Holies which was always kept entirely dark, this space is flooded

with light, the giant dome a single skylight. The hexagon's axis shifts as one enters, a private moment with sunlight coming in various directions. The atmosphere of the Hall is created from materials alone: chassagne beige limestone for paving, exposed concrete walls and columns, an inscription stone of black granite. Here is the minimalist integrity of metal shelves, engraved biblical texts on the walls, and large steps which also serve as seating, though nobody dares, though perhaps if one person sat others would follow.

An Eternal Flame burns, but does not act as centre. Rather it is the empty space in the middle, the polished nothing that draws attention. This void becomes the core of remembrance, the untouched middle becomes the axis at which people hesitate before daring to walk its blank breadth. If any space were guaranteed to produce *betroffen*, the German concept of being reduced to silence by guilt, speechless with shame, this would be it. The room is only ruined, aesthetically, by one problem. A wheelchair lift to carry the disabled to the floor. Clearly there are other more discreet solutions to this problem, a ramp could have been worked in more subtly. But the very brutality of this lift in the polished, perfect auditorium seems deliberate. Freed made certain this was more accessible than any comparable museum.

Freed reminds us that we can never expect an ideal, controlled environment without exclusion. We could gain the sterile victory of this space only by leaving out those who cannot climb steps, the physically imperfect targets of Nazi policy. Here we have true 'remembrance'. To remember that aesthetics cannot be divorced from ethics, that access to the event, real

87 Concourse level and stairs.
88–90 Sketches of the Hall of Remembrance by James Ingo Freed.
91, 92 Hall of Remembrance: long thin windows separate each of the six walls of the Hall (91), while in the corners, triangular motifs are cut out of the stone (92).

91

92

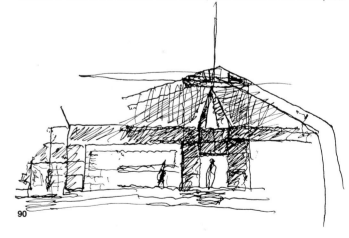

90

93

democracy, is more important than the ideal work of art. Access to all areas for all people is a crucial political point within architecture, the most literal, practical embodiment of democratic ideals.[18]

Conclusion

In the Holocaust Memorial Museum Freed has synthesized ('freed' even) a set of architectural gestures to produce a non-exclusive, non-hierarchic space that never proclaims the identity of the architect over the themes it serves. This is not a 'star' building, with an identifiable signature style, but in its democracy it resembles those artefacts created not by an individual, but by the pressures and context of history; by an era rather than an artist. If the judgement of Richard von Weizsacker, President of Germany, appears judiciously exaggerated – 'The most impressive place I have ever seen' – the museum will remain vital, whether the architect's name is remembered or not. Freed has made a building for history, memory, not for his own glory.

The museum performs that most difficult of task of telling us what took place in the past and of giving us some personal sense – physical not intellectual – of that experience: 'To know it as if it happened to us', to quote the Passover refrain. Freed knows that not all architecture can tell stories, but to say it has no message is equally wrong. If he played architectural games his intention would be lost, but he could not afford to refuse all narratives and retreat into hermetic good taste. In this balance between abstraction and representation Freed continues a long battle within Judaism itself about embellishment. After all,

after Herod had set up a golden eagle over the temple entrance, pious Jews objected and climbed up to smash it.

In this museum, Freed has produced a building that every contemporary debate about Modernism and post-modernism ends with: a call for architecture beyond categories, sufficiently good in its own right to supersede labels. A building analogous to the operations of memory, a form which always seems to have been there, familiar yet unique, never nostalgic yet essentially historical, modern whilst literally containing the past.

In trying to describe this building, to relate it to Modernism, neo-classicism, historicism, the best comparison that could be made might be with another recent Holocaust Memorial that has proved as much a popular success as Freed's museum: Henryk Górecki's Third Symphony.[19] This music is not Modernist yet is far from fake classicism, something utterly new created of tradition. You would not describe such work as new or old, modern or post-modern, you would only have to admit to how effective it is, entirely regardless of generic categorization.

As well as the ideal resolution of an almost impossible brief, the United States Holocaust Memorial Museum also suggests an alternative to our current architectural stalemate, a building unafraid of narrative yet never reliant on historicism, poetic whilst practical, operating through association rather than quotation, humble despite its scale and import. Freed's building is the model not only for all such museums and memorials but for a future in which serious, sophisticated architecture and popular success are finally reconciled.

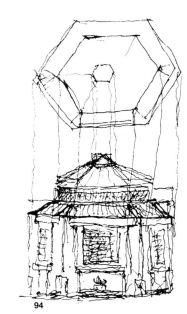
94

95

96

93 Hall of Remembrance skylight.
94 The hexagonal remembrance Hall, sketch by Freed.
95, 96 View of the Hall of Remembrance. Rows of candles and an Eternal Flame flicker in the stillness of this empty, contemplative space.

From the Eisenhower Plaza entrance the Holocaust Memorial Museum makes a continuum with the pre-existent buildings on either side but subverts both their materials and design for its own purposes, pulling them together whilst holding them apart. That the museum is based on the combination of seemingly contradictory elements – whether limestone and brick or the tower and the hexagon – makes it impossible to reduce the totality to a programmatic formula. The modesty of the entrance on this side is a deliberate contrast to the facade on 14th Street, continuing that play between the democratic and the necessarily monumental.

Resembling niches for statues or even places to hide, the breaks between the walls of the Hall of Witness makes each of them appear an independent, sculptural screen, comparable to Ellsworth Kelly's all-white canvases within the museum itself. What seems from without a sign of incompletion and fracture, for a topic that requires humility and uncertainty rather than completion, from within the Hall of Witness becomes a mystic element, the source of light, the illumination of the inner star of the chamber. The broken perfection of the exterior hexagon is also a source of the light needed to complete the atmosphere of the interior.

With the most rigorously simple details the museum maintains its austere dignity. The empty limestone panels on the exterior wall of the Hall of Remembrance use the warmth and texture of their materials to grant a sense of loss and silence from nothing more than sunlight and shadow.

THE THINGS I SAW BEGGAR DESCRIPTION . . . THE VISUAL EVIDENCE AND THE VERBAL TESTIMONY OF STARVATION, CRUELTY AND BESTIALITY WERE SO OVERPOWERING . . . . I MADE THE VISIT DELIBERATELY, IN ORDER TO BE IN A POSITION TO GIVE FIRST-HAND EVIDENCE OF THESE THINGS IF EVER, IN THE FUTURE, THERE DEVELOPS A TENDENCY TO CHARGE THESE ALLEGATIONS TO PROPAGANDA.

GENERAL DAVID EISENHOWER
SUPREME COMMANDER OF THE ALLIED FORCES
OHRDRUF CONCENTRATION CAMP
APRIL 15, 1945

32

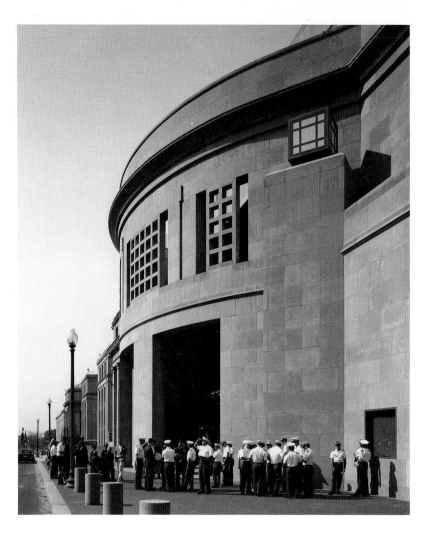

The monumental 14th Street entrance with all the renewed novelty of symmetry including the powerful positioning of outsize lamps. The proximity of the curved facade to the edge of the pavement and the strength of this geometric emphasis dominates the streetscape, imposing the building upon even the casual passer-by, to force the history of the Holocaust onto an otherwise banal thoroughfare.

This bold facade deceptively builds up the volume of the museum to grandiose proportions, only subsequently to subvert expectations of either pomp or symmetry: Neo-classical forms satisfy the most traditional visitors and then surprise them by transformations wrought within.

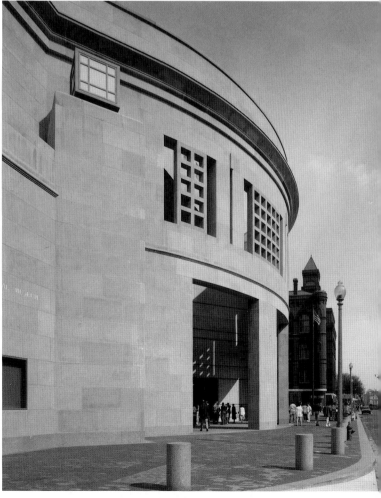

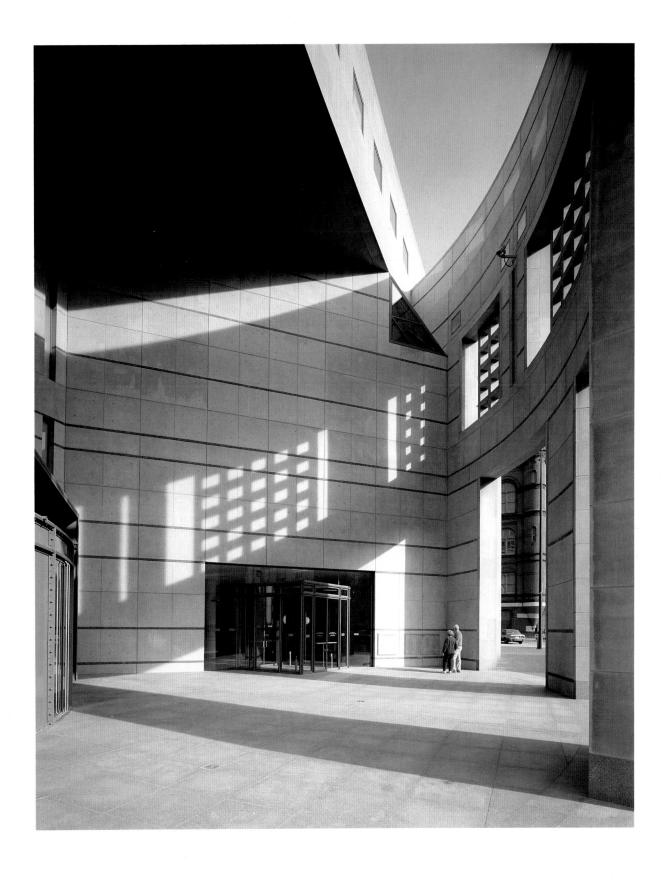

The first surprise for any visitor is in the realization of how much of a barrier and screen the facade acts as; immediately behind it lies a void, a shockingly empty space. If the facade in itself is imposing in its formal iconography, the open-air space it conceals is impressive and daunting by volume alone. Having entered through the facade the visitor is still outside, the certainties of the monumental entrance giving way to the ambiguity of emptiness and the necessity to make a choice between two, comparatively small doors. The functional metal details of the doors contrasts with the nobility and scale of the limestone, the industrial and the artisanal – twin themes of the building's materials here first stated. The cast shadow of the facade already suggests the theme of imprisonment.

36

A sense of disorientation is given further emphasis in views down the Hall of Witness, where a variety of freestanding metal elements act as one more form of entrance way, a sense of purpose then lost in the empty space of the Hall beyond. We are led down metal steps and out once more into an open field in which we must make our own directional decisions. If the twisted perspective of the skylight above is not immediately apparent, the shadows cast by it across the walls help break up further what is already a fragmentary spatial experience.

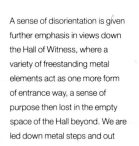

Views of the Hall of Witness make clear the complexity of the numerous elements at play. The seeming logic of the grand staircase up to the second floor is interfered with in reception by the Cubist jumble of the skylight above it. A sense of mounting towards unspecified threat is emphasized by the stark metal gates and light behind them. The sharp variety of moods conjured by the interplay of angles and edges is seen clearly with the aggressive intervention of Serra's sculpture (right), bifurcating the stairs with brutal simplicity.

The visual link between the peak of the Washington Monument and the shape of the roof is made all the clearer by night, tying the roof form not only to camp guardtowers but also to the surrounding civic topography. The bridges are practical yet clear in their metaphoric associations. Names of destroyed townships function as both a list of crimes, unafraid of literalism, and in shadow, reflection or abstraction as a patterned grid, simultaneously decorative and bluntly stern.

The distorted composition of the skylight is only fully comprehensible from the walkway bridges on the west side of the museum, which grant a completely different impression of the apparently logical space below. Here one also becomes conscious of the bridges above, reserved only for those granted access to the fifth floor. One is perhaps being witnessed from these other bridges whilst witnessing people in the Hall below. History and memory are made palpable in the form of glass etched with titles of destroyed towns, a transparent screen of recollection through which we can view the building and its occupants, dead names thrown upon us as shadows by the light.

The Tower of Victims is filled with photographs of residents of a destroyed *shetl*, narrowing up towards the illumination above as if literally 'moving into the light'. To be walked through on two floors, the Tower conveys an oppressive sensation of being surrounded by people on all sides, living and dead, with the weight and noise of other visitors walking right over one's head through the semi-transparent bridge. The mass of images, all of individuals, is even more effective due to the popularity and occasional overcrowding of the museum – our path narrows and we walk as a crowd through this absent crowd of ghosts. Downstairs, the Education Center is faced by a mural of tiles on the Holocaust theme designed by schoolchildren. Through the gap we can appreciate the relation of the Hall of Witness to the concourse level, which acts as negative space beneath it.

The stairway down to the concourse level in the Hall of Witness (above) mimics the form of the stairs to the second floor, but as a sombre version of the other's blatant theatricality. These grave stairs lead one straight down into Serra's sculpture, *Gravity*, which then splits you in either of two directions.

Wall drawings by Sol LeWitt (top right) create an atmosphere of repose and contemplation, one of the essential breaks from the pressure of the Holocaust's narrative. Abstract art and luxurious emptiness create decompression chambers during one's painful progress through an abundance of unbearable images. The narrow lifts provide the one, restrictive entrance to the museum exhibits (bottom right).

Every detail and element of the building operates both as metaphor and aesthetic solution, as here in the Hall of Remembrance where the triangular motif to be seen elsewhere reappears, cut out of the solid geometry of the limestone. The triangle is not only logical to the structure of this section but also functions as a part of the Star of David, the triangle forced on prisoners in the camps and a fraction of the number six repeated in the division and dimensions of the Hall. The selective play of exterior light adds further potency to the dramatic configuration of the Hall of Remembrance, whose bold massing of grand materials never detracts from its tranquillity.

The Hall of Remembrance is divided by the strength of daylight through narrow glass window strips that act as fissures to the unity of the chamber and turn each wall into a freestanding sculptural plane. The Eternal Flame and rows of candles provide flickers of hope in what is otherwise a sombre, tomblike interior.

The emptiness and rich minimalism of the materials creates a religious experience heightened, as well as musically spaced, by the shafts of light allowed in from without. By contemporary building standards to have created so large a volume dedicated to, and decorated with, nothing at all is a spiritual act in itself.

FOR THE DEAD AND THE LIVING WE MUST BEAR WITNESS

The sheer generosity of the Hall of Remembrance is in its simplicity of form, the six-sided Star of David, the six million dead, a shape of universal resonance, which only needs ordinary daylight and elegantly empty materials – limestone, granite and sandblasted steel – to demand that visitors be just as generous with their spirit. To step down into the silence and coldness of the floor becomes a moral act for each individual, unprotected by the company of others or reassurance of domestic objects.

Location plan

1 The United States
Holocaust Memorial Museum
2 White House
3 Lincoln Memorial
4 Jefferson Memorial
5 United States Capitol
6 Washington Monument
7 National Gallery of Art
8 National Archives
9 Museum of Natural History
10 Museum of American
History
11 Smithsonian Institute
12 Bureau of Engraving and
Printing
13 Freer Gallery
14 Hirshhorn Museum
15 Air and Space Museum

Drawings

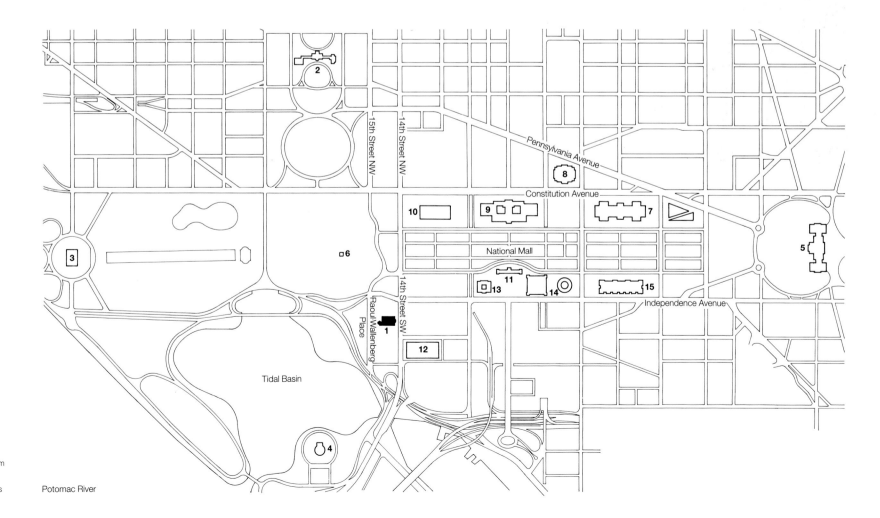

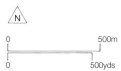

0   500m

0   500yds   Potomac River

Plans and Section

1 Meyerhoff Theater
2 theatre lobby
3 green room
4 amphitheatre
5 stairs to Hall of Witness
6 Education/Conference Center
7 classrooms
8 cinema
9 lift lobby
10 Temporary Exhibition Space
11 entrance for individuals
12 group entrance
13 stage
14 Hall of Flags
15 Hall of Witness
16 15th Street entrance
17 Patrons' Lounge
18 cloakroom
19 bookshop
20 loading dock
21 Permanent Exhibition Space
22 ante-chamber
23 Hall of Remembrance
24 Galleria
25 Hall of Learning
26 Tower of Victims

50

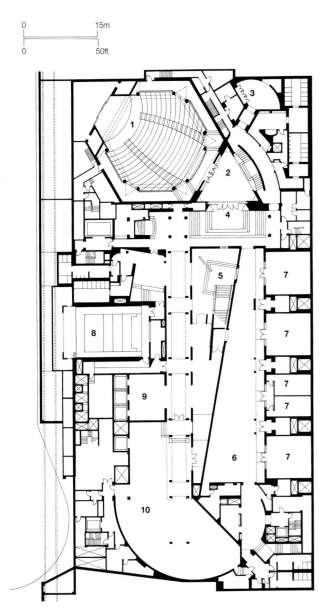

Concourse level

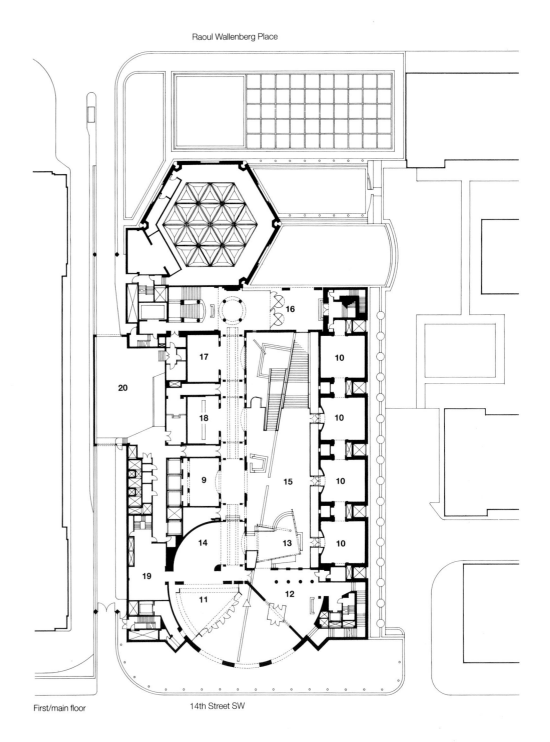

Raoul Wallenberg Place

First/main floor   14th Street SW

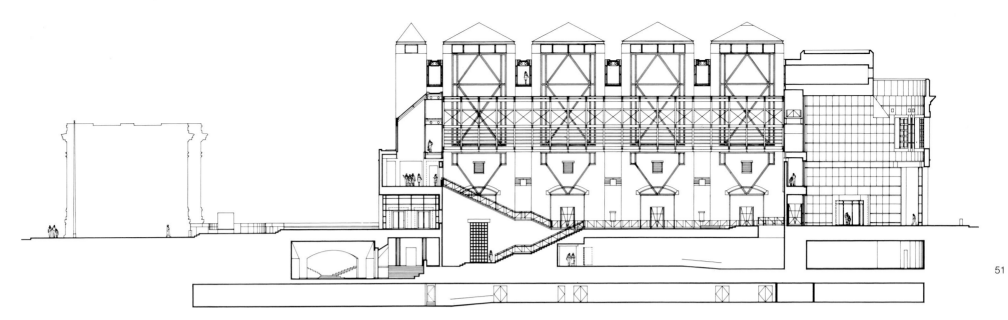

Longitudinal west–east section

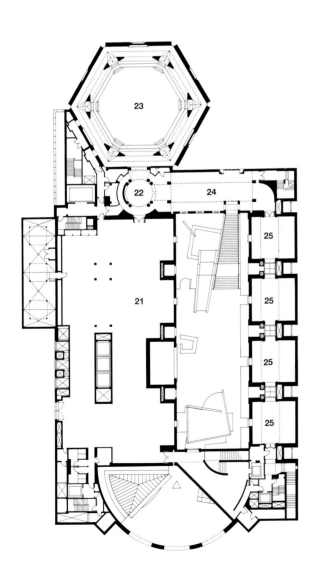

Second floor

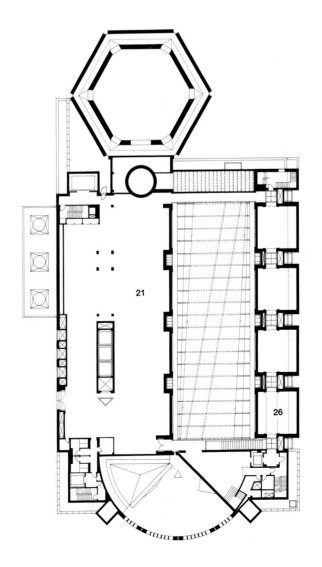

Third floor

Longitudinal east–west section

Plans and Sections

1 Permanent Exhibition Space
2 Tower of Victims
3 library/archives
4 administration
5 conference room
6 Survivors' Registry

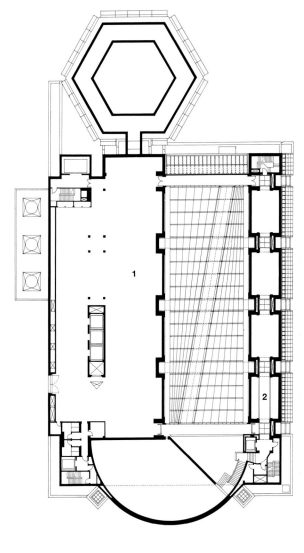

0   15m

0   50ft

Fourth floor

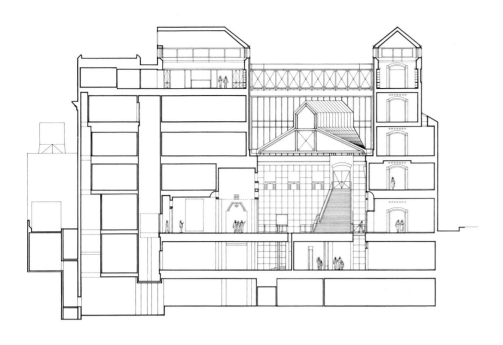

Cross section through Hall of Witness

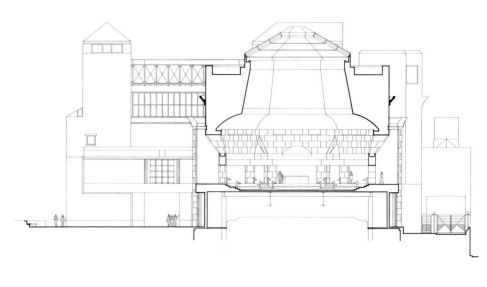

Cross section through Hall of Remembrance
(Meyerhoff Theater below)

0		10m
0		30ft

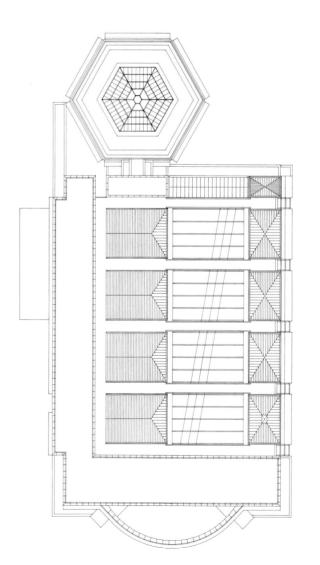

Fifth floor

Roof

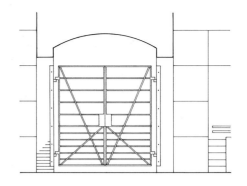
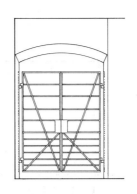
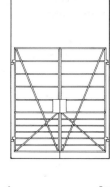

0   5m

0   15ft

Hall of Witness gate

1 2⅜in (60.3mm) diameter outer steel cylinder ¼in (6.35mm) thick made up of separate sections
2 continuous inner steel cylinder welded to ¼in (6.35mm) folded steel plate support
3 ¼in (6.35mm) steel plate 5¼in (133.35mm) high welded to gate vertical and outer steel cylinder
4 steel rod gate stabilizer
5 ⅜in (9.65mm) steel plate at floor
6 ¼in (6.35mm) folded steel plate gate pivot/railing supports bolted to concrete slab
7 granite paving
8 ¼in (6.35mm) steel plate 5¼in (133.35mm) high welded to outer steel cylinder and bolted to steel angles
9 1½ x 1½ x ¼in (38.1 x 38.1 x 6.35mm) steel angles welded to steel floor plate
10 concrete floor slab

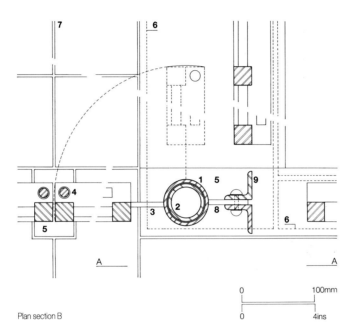

0   100mm

0   4ins

Plan section B

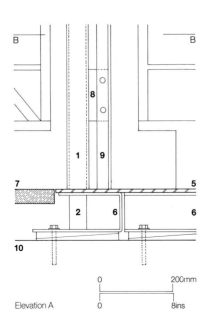

0   200mm

0   8ins

Elevation A

Hall of Witness gate

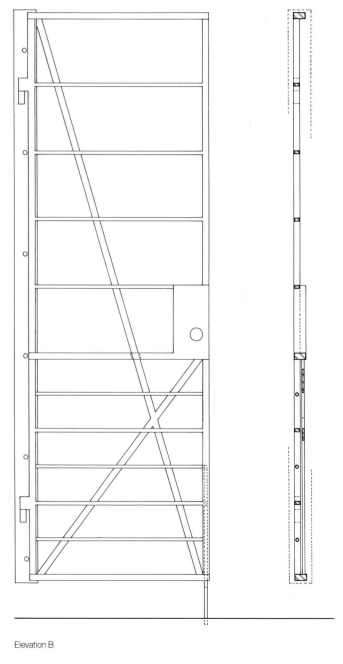

Elevation B

0   500mm

0   20ins

Typical gate

**Typical fifth floor bridge and
exhibition bridges**

Section details

1 cruciform hanger assembly:
   3 x 3 x ½in (76.2 x 76.2 x
   12.7mm) angle, ½in
   (12.7mm) plate, and ¾in
   (19mm) diameter bolts
2 insulated aluminium glazing
   unit: patterned surface to
   one pane of glass
3 7⅝ x 7⅝ x 3½in (193.7 x
   193.7 x 88.9mm) glass
   block with sandblasted
   top surface
4 stainless steel hexagon head
   bolt, 4 per cruciform
5 1¾in (44.45mm) diameter
   steel rod bracing
6 shop-applied structural
   silicon bead and back-up
   tape
7 weatherproof silicon
   sealant and backer rod
8 weep tube, two per frame
9 continuous neoprene strip
10 built-up exposed structural
   steel box girder
11 exposed architectural
   concrete

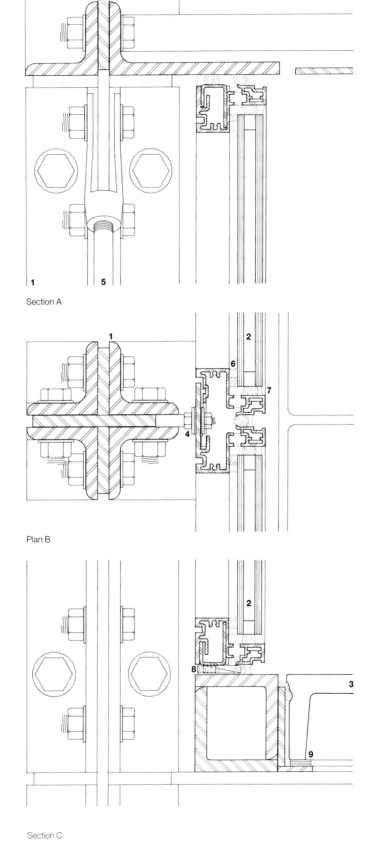

Section A

Plan B

Section C

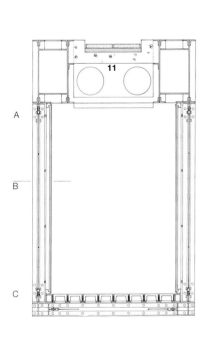

0 ————————— 1m

0 ————————— 3ft

Details

0 ————————— 100m

0 ————————— 4ins

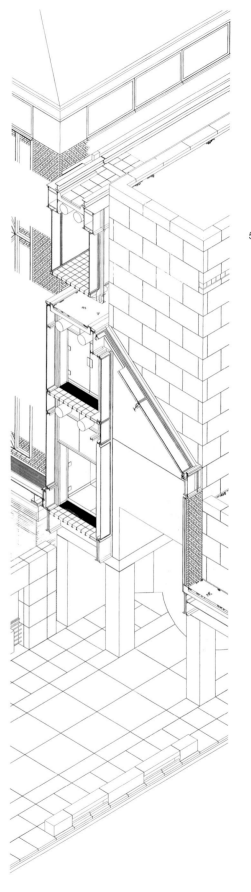

55

Isometric section

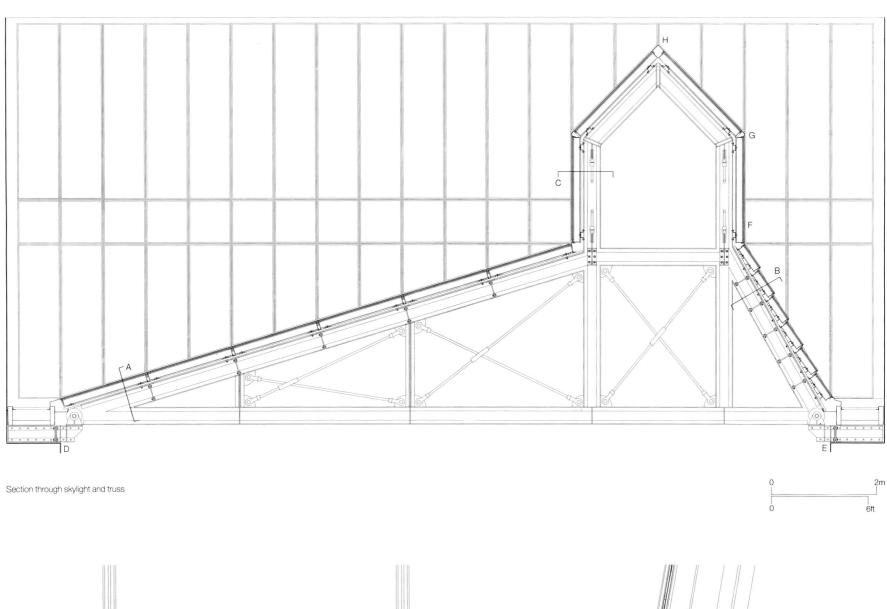

Section through skylight and truss

```
0                    2m
|___|___|___|___|___|
0                   6ft
```

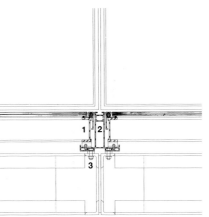

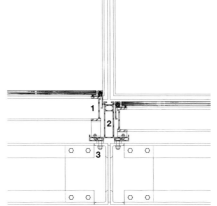

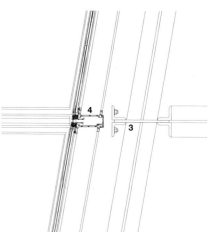

Plan-section A

Plan-section B

Plan-section C

Skylight section details

1 glazing unit for sloping portion of skylight (114 different sizes, two of each): $1^{13}/_{64}$in (20.64mm) heat strengthened glass
2 extruded aluminium rafter for sloping portion of skylight
3 typical truss assembly: 3 x 3 x $^{1}/_{2}$in (76.2 x 76.2 x 12.7mm) angle, $^{1}/_{2}$in (12.7mm) plate, and $^{3}/_{4}$in (19mm) diameter bolts
4 glazing unit for vertical portion of skylight monitor: $1^{13}/_{64}$in (20.64mm) heat strengthened glass
5 skylight truss pin connection
6 internal gutter
7 end cap
8 painted aluminium grating
9 aluminium clad and neoprene lined gutter
10 #5 clevis
11 glazing unit for sloping portion of skylight monitor: $1^{13}/_{64}$in (20.64mm) heat strengthened glass
12 eaves cap
13 ridge cap

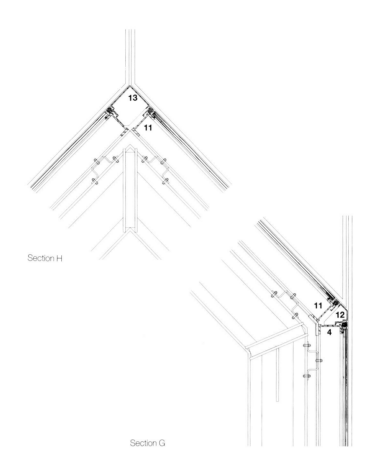

Section H

Section G

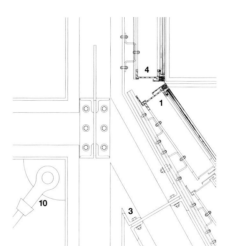

Section F

| 0 | | 500mm |
| 0 | | 20ins |

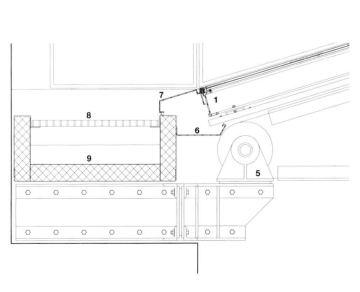

Section D

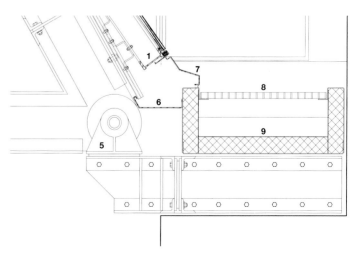

Section E

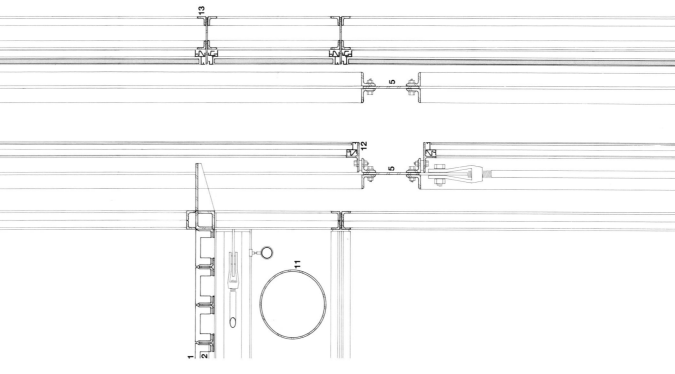

Section details

1 7⅝ x 7⅝ x 3½in (193.7 x 193.7 x 88.9mm) glass block with sandblasted top surface

2 steel T-glass block support

3 sprinkler pipe

4 brick arch

5 typical skylight truss assembly: 3 x 3 x ½in (76.2 x 76.2 x 12.7mm) angle, ½in (12.7mm) plate, and ¾in (19mm) diameter bolts

6 typical west end wall structural member: 2 x 2 x ⅜in (50.8 x 50.8 x 9.53mm) angle and ⅜in (9.53mm) plate. Plug welds in angles are ¹¹/₁₆in (17.46mm) diameter, ⅜in (9.53mm) thick, and at 4in (101.6mm) centres. Exposed surfaces ground flush and smooth

7 continuous neoprene seal

8 end wall insulated glazing unit: patterned surface to one pane of glass

9 1½in (38.1mm) diameter bracing rod

10 west end wall monitor glazing unit: ½in (12.7mm) clear annealed glass

11 supply air duct

12 cut steel T-frame for west end wall monitor glazing

13 typical east end wall structural member

14 1³⁄₁₆in (30.16mm) insulated aluminium panel

15 expansion joint

16 skylight rafter aluminium extrusion

17 skylight glazing unit: ¹³⁄₁₆in (20.64mm) clear heat strengthened glass

18 painted gypsum board suspended ceiling

19 structural bracing at top of east end wall

20 ³⁄₁₆in (4.76mm) painted aluminium panel, with aluminium foil faced insulation

21 exposed steel channel

22 typical fifth floor bridge cruciform hanger

23 painted aluminium grating

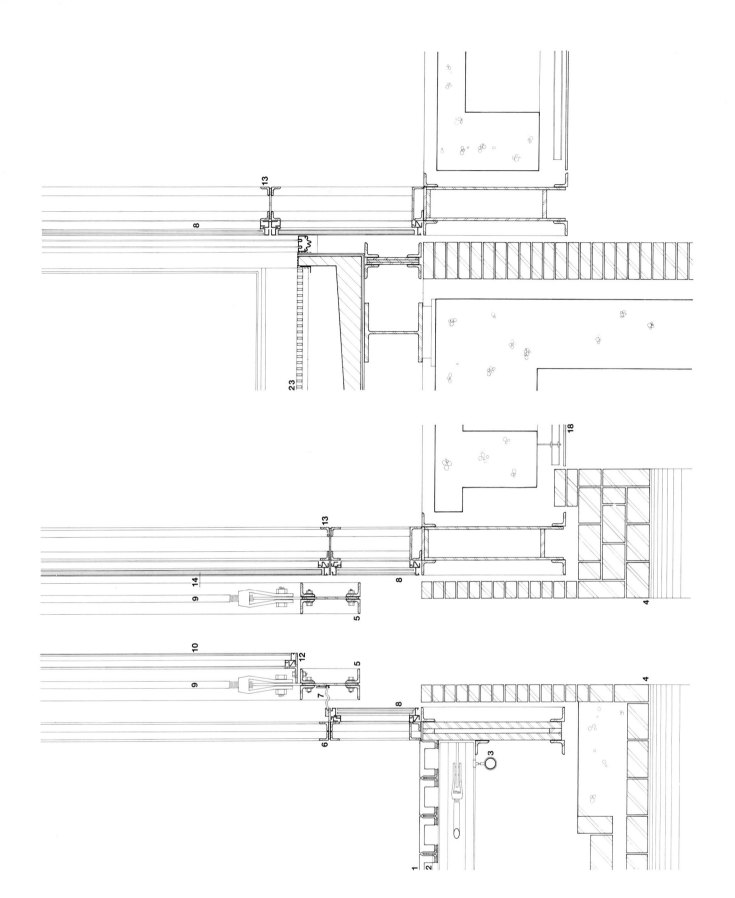

Section through east end wall
at third and fifth floors

Section through east end wall
at third and fourth floors

Section through west end wall
at third and fourth floors

500mm

20ins

0

0

Author's acknowledgements

All my thanks to James Ingo Freed for his very generous time, patience and confidence. Thanks to Stephen Robinson in Washington for his hospitality and to Joseph Semah in Amsterdam for initial discussions of Judaism and architecture. Thanks to my father, the architect Trevor Dannatt, for all he ever showed me about buildings; and thanks to Paul Finch for publishing my original essay in *Building Design*.

Illustration acknowledgements

The following illustrations have been provided courtesy of the following: figs 8, 9: Jeff Goldberg / ESTO; fig 10: George Cserna; figs 11, 12, 16, 19, 23: Nathaniel Lieberman; fig 25: Peter Aaron / ESTO; fig 26: Geoff Renner; figs 44, 45: Maxwell Mackenzie. All other photography of the United States Holocaust Memorial Museum by Timothy Hursley.

60

Notes

1 Theodor Adorno, *Engagement*, *Noten Zur Literatur III* (Frankfurt: Suhrkamp Verlag, 1965).

2 George Steiner, *Language and Silence* (New York: Atheneum, 1967).

3 'The character of the building itself had an almost unintended link to fascist architecture.' Charles H Atherton, Executive Secretary Fine Arts Commission, 1986.

4 Yehuda Amichai, 'Damascus Gate' in *Selected Poems*, trans Chana Bloch (New York: Harper & Row, 1986).

5 There are plentiful examples of classic Modernist buildings taken over and used by the Nazis for processing or torture, exploiting the logic of their programme. From Drancy's Vélodrome d'Hiver, 70,000

French Jews were sent to death camps. The buildings were designed as worker housing by progressive architects of the 1930s, standardized structures Nazis found ideal for their purposes. Erich Mendelsohn's Columbushaus (1929–30), a Bauhaus archetype, was leased by the Gestapo and then the SS, and whose practical modern design was ideal for a political detention centre.

6 *A+U*, February 1988.

7 'Recess for a doorway or window' is the dictionary definition of 'ingoing' as in 'ingoings of all the doors, or other openings in thick walls, to be finished with linings', 'ingoings of all the windows… to be finished with linings', Donaldson & Glen, *Specifications*, 1859. The curious architectural associations of James Freed's middle name should not go unremarked, somehow allied to his own use of metaphor: 'ingo; obsolete, "to go in, to enter". "Hu maez man ingan on stranges hus" c 1000, Gosp Matt XII 29', *OED*. The other architectural link: Inigo Jones was the son of a clothmaker, also called Inigo. Presumably Inigo and Ingo are not etymologically too far apart.

8 Debórah Dwork and Robert Jan van Pelt, 'Reclaiming Auschwitz', in *Holocaust Remembrance* (London: Blackwell, 1994).

9 Lebbeus Woods, *War and Architecture*, Pamphlet Architecture 15 (New York: Princeton Architectural Press, 1993).

10 Freed would have liked to leave construction unfinished at its base, fearing it might appear too clean, resolved at this point. Architect Peter Eisenman's only request to Freed was that this building should never be finished.

11 Jean-François Lyotard, *Heidegger and 'The Jews'* (University of Minnesota Press, 1990).

12 The cattle car in the permanent exhibition, donated by Polish State Railways, has four metal slats on the side, facing down, which make a comparison with the light fixtures in the Hall of Witness overt.

13 Steve Reich's *Different Trains* could be mentioned in this context, and the application of a supposedly non-illustrative form of contemporary music, 'Minimalism', to suggest a storyline, outline a narrative. The congruity between the repetitive Minimalist beat and the sound of the trains that led to the death camps, creates an opportunity to reintroduce content to an otherwise abstract format. A comparison could be made with Freed's

careful use of materials, practical in themselves, to suggest elements of the Holocaust.

14 Amichai, *op cit*.

15 This sense of seeing the shapes of the Holocaust in everything is described by Melvin Charney in *The German Series*: 'The compelling presence of the extermination camps infiltrates my work. Every building I look at or image I conceive reveals ovens, chimneys, barracks and body racks.'

16 Among the many artists who worked directly with the museum, or helped inspire it, was James Cathcart. An architect-artist he previously disassembled a house in Detroit and reassembled it in an art gallery, as well as installing public toilets in the facade of Storefront, the New York gallery. Cathcart took down the Birkenau stable and reassembled it in the museum. For this he analysed the 40-year old structure closely. The stable was systematically built, a smart system of construction, peg-notched, wall bearing, almost interchangeable with Modernist traditions. Drawings were done by Germans, it was built by Polish Jews in camp. Cathcart hired three carpenters, took the bits to a warehouse, then reassembled it. He considers it a work of art in itself, as a process, albeit a morally very ambiguous one.

17 Aldo Rossi, *A Scientific Autobiography* (New York: Oppositions Books, 1981), p 65.

18 Since Dianne Pilgrim of Cooper-Hewitt National Museum of Design developed MS, she has become committed to demonstrating the full socio-political meaning of design, the ideology of access, and how it affects every aspect of our lives, especially wheelchair users such as herself.

19 Górecki was born three years after Freed in 1933. Symphony No 3, 'Symphony of Sorrowful Songs', is dedicated to the memory of Oswiecim or Auschwitz near the village where Górecki was born and his present home at Katowice. David Drew's notes for the bestselling Elektra Nonesuch recording make explicit the architectural metaphors within this music: 'For the unprejudiced listener of any kind, and also for the specialist whose musicality can still get the better of his or her prejudices, it is not a work that calls for 'elucidation'; the light it sheds at first hearing is exceptionally bright and direct…'

Select bibliography

A+U, No 278, November 1993

Assemblage, No 9, June 1989 (Cambridge, MA: MIT Press)

Blake, P, *The Master Builders* (New York: Norton, 1976)

Hartman, G H (ed), *Holocaust Remembrance* (Cambridge, Blackwell, 1994)

Hilberg, R, *The Destruction of the European Jews* (New York: Holmes & Meier, 1985)

Jewish Affairs, July 1992, Vol 47, No 2, Johannesburg

Johnson, Paul, *A History of the Jews* (London: Weidenfeld and Nicholson, 1987)

Kultur Chronik, 1/1989, Bonn

Mies van der Rohe, *Critical Essays* (New York: MOMA and MIT Press, 1989). Includes interview with Freed on Mies in America and Richard Pommer's 'Mies and the Political Ideology of the Modern Movement in Architecture'

Milton, S, *In Fitting Memory* (Detroit: Wayne State University Press, 1991)

Speer, A, *Architektur* (Berlin: Propylaen, 1978)

Wiseman, C, *I M Pei* (New York: Harry N Abrams, 1990)

Young, James, E, *The Texture of Memory: Holocaust Memorials and Meaning* (New Haven: Yale University Press, 1993)

Young, James, E, *Writing and Rewriting the Holocaust: Narrative and the Consequences of Interpretation* (Bloomington: Indiana University Press, 1988)

Chronology

Preliminary discussions: July 1985
Planning commenced: October 1986
Construction commenced: July 1989
Public dedication: April 22 1993

Statistics

Museum
90' 0" high (5 floors above grade/2 below)
Hall of Remembrance: 6,000 ft²
Hall of Witness: 7,500 ft²
Permanent exhibition space (on levels 2–4): 36,000 ft²
Temporary exhibition space (on level 1 and concourse): 8,000 ft²
Hall of Learning (level 2): 3,600 ft²
Education/Conference Center (concourse) 4,318 ft²
Library/Archives/Research Center: 16,000 ft²
Meyerhoff Theater (concourse) 5,486 ft² (414 fixed seats)
Cinema (concourse): 2,073 ft² (178 fixed seats)
Bookshop: 1,295 ft²
Annex: 45,000 ft² (renovated by Notter Feingold & Alexander)
Gross building area 258,000 ft²
Site area 75,512 ft² (1.7 acres)
Foundation Cast-in-place reinforced concrete spread footings

Structure

Main building (towers) Cast-in-place concrete framing and bearing walls from concourse level to roof; steel gable-roof framing and supporting framing at each tower. Moulded brick walls are self-supporting

East end Concrete and metal deck slab and steel framing at fifth floor and roof

Hall of Witness Steel trusses supporting the skylight

Hall of Remembrance Steel framing, with a cast-in-place reinforced concrete slab at second floor; precast concrete-encased steel columns; steel framing at skylight roof and sides of Hall; cast-in-place reinforced concrete exterior walls, supporting the limestone cladding

Facade

Indiana limestone and cedar rose granite with steel or concrete backup; moulded brick with precast concrete lintels and grey painted aluminium angle inserts; architectural concrete (with brick inset at 14th Street entrance); architectural exposed structural steel with grey paint, clear glass in grey painted aluminium frames; aluminum panels painted grey; lead coated copper roofs at towers and entry pavilion

Exterior paving

Modular brick paving with cedar rose granite borders and curbs

Interior finishes

Major public spaces: Cedar rose granite, moulded brick or wool carpet floors; moulded brick walls with precast concrete lintels

Hall of Witness Cedar rose granite paving with glass block floor inset, moulded brick or wool carpet floors; moulded brick walls with precast concrete lintels and painted ornamental steel; black granite and white marble end walls; grey painted structural steel bridges and trusses supporting clear glass hyperbolic paraboloid skylight and ceramic frit patterned glass window walls in grey painted frames

Hall of Remembrance Chassagne beige limestone and prato fiorito granite paving; architectural concrete outer walls with Chassagne beige limestone insets and sandblasted steel candle recesses; Indiana limestone inner walls with architectural concrete lintels; painted plaster ceiling and clear glass skylights in grey painted aluminium frames with translucent laylight glass

Meyerhoff Theater Wood stage floor, wool carpet aisles and stairs, troweled composition flooring below seating; precast concrete walls with perforated metal panel insets; precast concrete ceiling; steel and glass acoustic canopy

Cinema Wood platform floor, wool carpet aisles and stairs, troweled composition flooring below seating; gypsum drywall partitions with

perforated metal panel insets; perforated metal panel ceiling with gypsum wallboard perimeter

Mechanical

Central electric refrigeration plant provides the cooling medium; heating is provided by electricity. Entire museum heated and cooled by all air systems (excepting entrance cabinet heaters) utilizing combination of VAV systems, constant volume reheat systems and humidification control for special areas, galleries and administration areas. Individual systems are provided for the Hall of Witness, Hall of Remembrance, theatre and general gallery areas

Vertical circulation

Elevators (8): 6 passenger (4 hydraulic, 2 electric); 1 service (electric); 1 freight elevator (hydraulic)

Stairs: 2 grand stairs, 5 fire stairs

Architects and consultants

Client
United States Holocaust Memorial Council

Pei Cobb Freed & Partners' Services
Architectural; Interior Design

Project team
James Ingo Freed, *Partner-in-charge/Design*
Werner Wandelmaier, *Partner/Administration*
Michael D Flynn, *Partner/Technology*
Craig Dumas, *Associate Partner/Administration*
Beatrice Lehman, *Associate Partner/Production*
Michael Vissichelli, *Senior Associate/Production*
Harry Barone, *Senior Associate/Site Architect*
Wendy Evans Joseph, *Senior Associate/Design*
Marek Zamdmer, *Senior Associate/Design*
Jean-Pierre Mutin, *Associate/Design*
Stephen Ohnemus, *Associate/Administration*
Jou Min Lin, *Building Envelope*
Alissa Bucher, *Associate*
Abby Suckle, *Associate/Interiors*
Deborah Campbell, *Associate/Theatres*
Anne Lewison, Jeff Stumacher, Steven Valentine, Jeffrey Rosenberg, Leslie Neblett, Ray Lee, Howard Settles, Fritz Sulzer, Gianni Neri, Christine Mahoney. Jennifer Adler, Paul Albrecht, Marcos Alvarez, Giovanna Brancaccio, Quin Chen, John Coburn, Monica Coe, Karen Cox, Steven Derasmo, Paul Drago, Richard Dunham, Richard Gorman, Rossana Gutierrez, David Harmon, Reginald Hough, Kevin Johns, Jennifer Nadler, Michael Ngu, Camillo Rosales, Amiel Savaldi, Emily Sidorsky, Mercedes Stadthagen, Deborah Taylor, Hieu Vuong

Associate architect
Notter Feingold & Alexander, Washington, D C
George Notter, *Partner-in-Charge*; Manuel Almagro, *Project Manager*

General contractor
Blake Construction Company, Washington, D C

Consultants
Structural Weiskopf & Pickworth, NYC; J Richard Savignano, *Associate*
Mechanical/electrical Cosentini Associates, New York, NY
Fire & life safety Rolf Jensen & Associates, Inc, Fairfax, VA
Lighting Jules Fisher/Paul Marantz, New York, NY
Theatre design Jules Fisher Associates, New York, NY
Acoustical Jaffe Acoustics, Norwalk, CT
Audio-visual Boyce Nemec Designs, Norwalk, CT
Elevators Calvin Kort, Inc, Glen Rock, NY
Soils engineering Woodward-Clyde Consultants, New York, NY
Landscape Hanna/Olin, Philadelphia, PA
Security Issco Corp, Westbury, CT
Planning (general) Taylor & Nakagawa, New York, NY
Cost consulting Scharf-Godfrey, Inc, New York, NY
Art Nancy Rosen, Inc, New York, NY

Major subcontractors
Excavation John Driggs C, Inc, Upper Marlboro, MD
Curtain wall Columbia Architectural Metals, Pittsburgh, PA
Skylights English Architectural Glazing Corp, Pennsauken, NJ
Masonry G-A Masonry Corporation, Crestwood, KY
Stone setting Roubin and Janiero, Inc, Fairfax, VA
Limestone Harding and Cogswell Corp, Bedford, IN
Stone Sopromat, Montreal, Canada
Ornamental metals Gichner/ Coastal Iron Works, Inc, Beltsville, MD
Structural steel Rome Iron Group Ltd, Rome, NY
Steel and precast erector Sterling/ICC, College Park, MD
Elevator Otis Elevator Company, Alexandria, VA

Artists
Ellsworth Kelly *Memorial*, installation, third–fourth floor lounge
Sol LeWitt *Consequence*, installation, second floor lounge
Richard Serra *Gravity*, Cor-ten steel sculpture installed on concourse stairs
Joel Shapiro *Loss and Regeneration*, two-part cast bronze in Raoul Wallenberg Place